D1359831

Performance-Enhancing Drugs

by Laura K. Egendorf

Drugs

ReferencePoint
Press™

San Diego, CA

© 2007 ReferencePoint Press, Inc.

For more information, contact
ReferencePoint Press, Inc.
PO Box 27779
San Diego, CA 92198
www. ReferencePointPress.com

Picture Credits:
AP/Wide World Photos, 12
Getty Images, 9, 16
Steve Zmina, 28–31, 42–44, 58–61, 72–75

Series design:
Tamia Dowlatabadi

LIBRARY OF CONGRESS CATALOGING-IN-PUBLICATION DATA

Egendorf, Laura K.
  Performance-enhancing drugs / by Laura K. Egendorf.
    p. cm. — (Compact research series)
  Includes bibliographical references and index.
  ISBN-13: 978-1-60152-003-6 (hardback)
  ISBN-10: 1-60152-003-4 (hardback)
  1. Doping in sports—Juvenile literature. I. Title.
  RC1230.N47 2006
  362.29—dc22

                                                      2006032343

Contents

Foreword

As modern civilization continues to evolve, its ability to create, store, distribute, and access information expands exponentially. The explosion of information from all media continues to increase at a phenomenal rate. By 2020 some experts predict the worldwide information base will double every 73 days. While access to diverse sources of information and perspectives is paramount to any democratic society, information alone cannot help people gain knowledge and understanding. Information must be organized and presented clearly and succinctly in order to be understood. The challenge in the digital age becomes not the creation of information, but how best to sort, organize, enhance, and present information.

ReferencePoint Press developed the Compact Research series with this challenge of the information age in mind. More than any other subject area today, researching current events can yield vast, diverse, and unqualified information that can be intimidating and overwhelming for even the most advanced and motivated researcher. The Compact Research series offers a compact, relevant, intelligent, and conveniently organized collection of information covering a variety of current and controversial topics ranging from illegal immigration to marijuana.

The series focuses on three types of information: objective single-author narratives, opinion-based primary source quotations, and facts and statistics. The clearly written objective narratives provide context and reliable background information. Primary source quotes are carefully selected and cited, exposing the reader to differing points of view. And facts and statistics sections aid the reader in evaluating perspectives. Presenting these key types of information creates a richer, more balanced learning experience.

For better understanding and convenience, the series enhances information by organizing it into narrower topics and adding design features that make it easy for a reader to identify desired content. For example, in *Compact Research: Illegal Immigration*, a chapter covering the economic impact of illegal immigration has an objective narrative explaining the various ways the economy is impacted, a balanced section of numerous primary source quotes on the topic, followed by facts and full-color illustrations to encourage evaluation of contrasting perspectives.

The ancient Roman philosopher Lucius Annaeus Seneca wrote, "It is quality rather than quantity that matters." More than just a collection of content, the Compact Research series is simply committed to creating, finding, organizing, and presenting the most relevant and appropriate amount of information on a current topic in a user-friendly style that invites, intrigues, and fosters understanding.

Performance-Enhancing Drugs at a Glance

Health Risks

Numerous health risks have been connected to performance-enhancing drugs. These effects range from acne and baldness to liver damage, stroke, and heart disease.

Steroid Use Among Teenagers

Evidence suggests the problem of performance-enhancing drugs is widespread, especially among teenagers. Some studies also suggest that nearly half of all steroid users are teenagers.

Legality

Many legal drugs can be considered performance enhancing. Steroids, for example, do have legitimate medical uses, such as helping accident victims redevelop atrophied muscles. Drugs that may be legally obtained are nevertheless often banned for use by athletes. In fact, some athletes may test positive for steroid use if they use certain over-the-counter cold medicines.

Blood Doping

Even though blood doping is a technique that uses a naturally occurring substance (red blood cells), it is still considered a performance enhancer because it gives the athlete an unfair advantage.

Effective Testing

Testing for performance-enhancing drugs can be effective only if it is administered fairly and frequently. Current debate among professional and amateur athletic organizations centers on how to define a fair testing protocol and how often the tests should be administered.

Avoiding Detection

Athletes who want to avoid detection during drug tests can use several methods. They may take a masking agent (a drug that hides the presence of performance-enhancing drugs), switch their urine with a clean sample, or carefully plan when they use the drugs to ensure that the drugs are out of their system prior to testing.

Is Using Performance-Enhancing Drugs Cheating?

Using performance-enhancing drugs can increase endurance and strength, reduce the time it takes to recover from injury, and help athletes deal with the focus and stress of competition. Any one of these factors can give an athlete an advantage he or she would not normally have.

Some people argue for the legalization of performance-enhancing drugs. They contend that making these drugs available to all athletes would level the playing field and turn performance-enhancing drugs into simply another training aid.

Overview: Performance-Enhancing Drugs in Modern Athletics

❝The use of performance enhancing drugs by . . . athletes has only recently become a public issue, though it has been a serious problem in the sports community for many years.❞

—Robert Voy, *Drugs, Sports and Politics,* 1991.

Few people are more admired in today's society than successful athletes. Adolescents view them as role models, adults clamor for their autographs, and companies seek them out to endorse products. While most athletes become successful as a result of their talent and hard work, others take medical shortcuts. To the dismay of fans, the medical community, and many athletes themselves, steroids and other performance-enhancing drugs have become a common element of modern sports.

What Are Performance-Enhancing Drugs?

Performance-enhancing drugs are substances or tactics used by athletes to improve their chances of winning competitions. The most common performance-enhancing drugs are anabolic-androgenic steroids. *Anabolic* means muscle-building, while *androgenic* refers to masculine characteristics. First developed in the 1930s, these drugs were created to mimic the effects of the male hormones testosterone and androtestosterone, which regulate the development of muscles and secondary male sex characteristics. Synthetic steroids were initially developed to assist people suffering from abnormally low levels of testosterone or from diseases that attack

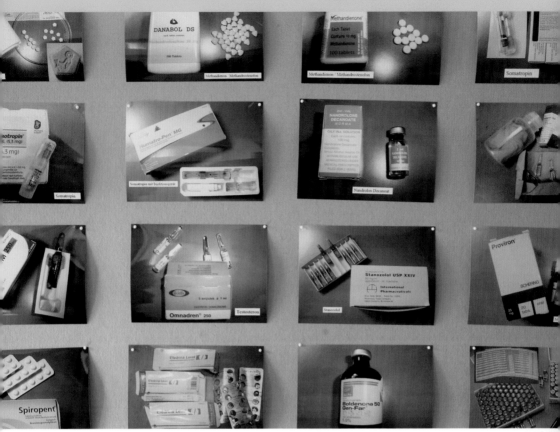

These photos of anabolic steroids are on display after a being seized in Germany. The most common performance-enhancing drugs are anabolic-androgenic steroids.

muscles. However, as often happens with new drugs, other uses were quickly found for them.

Athletes use anabolic steroids to increase muscle development and to reduce recovery time from injury. Steroids can be taken orally, injected, or applied topically as a cream. Different variants of the drugs are often used at the same time, a technique called stacking. Athletes stack steroids in an attempt to limit side effects while increasing the potency of the drugs. Steroid users typically take the drugs for a period of weeks or months, stop for a period of time, and then resume their use.

Another type of drug often abused by athletes are amphetamines. First developed in 1887, these drugs stimulate the body by spurring the release of the neural transmitters dopamine, serotonin, and noradrenaline. Amphetamines, known colloquially by athletes as "greenies," increase heart rate and blood pressure and stimulate the pleasure centers of the brain. They are found in legal pharmaceuticals such as diet pills and Ritalin, but also exist as the street drugs methamphetamine and speed. Athletes take amphetamines to compete longer and improve their concentration.

HGH and Blood Doping

Some practices that boost performance do not involve drugs at all. Two primary examples are blood doping and the use of human growth hormone (HGH). Athletes who dope their blood or use HGH often do so because these methods not only improve their skills but are also more natural and nearly impossible to detect.

Human growth hormone (HGH) is a naturally occurring substance secreted by the pituitary gland. HGH promotes cell growth in the body and the development of muscle, cartilage, and bone. Originally, the only way to obtain HGH was by extracting it from the pituitary glands of cadavers. Later, a synthetic version was developed. HGH is used to treat stunted growth in children and other growth-related diseases.

> **Athletes who use HGH or dope their blood often do so because these methods not only improve their skills but are also more natural and nearly impossible to detect.**

Athletes take HGH to increase muscle growth and to help tired muscles recover faster, making it possible for them to train longer and more frequently. Unlike other performance-enhancing drugs, HGH cannot be detected in urine; blood tests must be used to find the drug. Even with blood tests, however, it is often difficult to determine the difference between a naturally high level of HGH and one that has been artificially elevated.

The goal of blood doping is to increase the number of red blood cells in an athlete's body. Because red blood cells carry oxygen to the muscles, more red blood cells means more oxygen, which is beneficial to performance in endurance events such as long-distance cycling races. Blood doping is the removal and storage of blood from an athlete well in advance of a competition. Doing so prompts the body to replace the missing blood, bringing the level of red blood cells back up to normal. Then, just before an event, the athlete is transfused with the stored blood, boosting the number of red blood cells well above normal.

Higher levels of red blood cells can also be achieved by using erythropoietin (EPO). First isolated in 1977, this substance occurs naturally in the kidneys and is responsible for regulating the production of red blood cells. The medical purpose of EPO is to treat anemia patients; however, athletes use EPO instead of transfusions to elevate their red blood cell count.

> **Tests to detect EPO were not developed until 2000.**

Blood doping is very difficult to detect. If an athlete uses the transfusion method, tests will not reveal anything unnatural because no foreign substances will be discovered; the blood is entirely that of the athlete. Tests to detect EPO were not developed until 2000. Even now, a test can find manufactured EPO only if the test is administered within eight days of the athlete using the drug. The most common way for athletes to be caught blood doping is for EPO or stored blood to be found in their possession.

A Brief History of Performance-Enhancing Drugs

While they might seem like a modern issue, performance-enhancing drugs have been used throughout sports history. Athletes in ancient Greece ate sheep testicles and mushrooms in the belief that they would help their athletic endeavors. Roman gladiators used stimulants to increase their ability to fight. When cocaine was developed in the 19th century, athletes used it to improve their performance; runners and cyclists combined cocaine with heroin to increase their endurance. Such tactics were sometimes fatal. Morphine is believed to have caused the death of Welsh cyclist Arthur Lindon in 1896. In 1904 U.S. Olympian Tom Hicks collapsed and nearly died after winning the marathon. During the race, his trainers had given him a mixture of brandy, cocaine, and strychnine, a deadly poison.

The modern era of performance-enhancing drugs began in the 1930s. During that decade, scientists first isolated the male hormone testosterone,

A federal grand jury is currently investigating whether Barry Bonds committed perjury in 2003 when he testified that he had never used steroids. Athletes use anabolic steroids to increase muscle development and to reduce recovery time from injury.

and amphetamines were also developed at that time. According to the European Commission, an organization that enforces the European Union's ban on performance-enhancing drugs, amphetamines were first used for athletic purposes at the 1936 Summer Olympics. Baseball players have used amphetamines illegally since the 1960s. In the 1950s anabolic steroids were introduced to sports, initially at the 1956 World Games in Moscow. Steroid use also made its way into the Olympics. It was not until 1967 that the International Olympic Committee passed legislation that outlawed steroid use.

Performance-enhancing drugs have continued to evolve as technology advances, and drug testing is rarely able to keep pace. In the 1980s and 1990s new drugs were developed that were undetectable at the time. Perhaps not surprisingly, the use of these drugs, particularly during the

Olympic Games, exploded during this period. Some athletes, such as Canadian sprinter Ben Johnson, were caught using banned substances. Others, among them American sprinter Florence Griffith Joyner, never tested positive for any performance-enhancing drugs during the Olympics, but their remarkable success on the international stage raised considerable speculation. As Malcolm Gladwell contends in an article for the *New Yorker*:

> It is hard to believe . . . that the sprinter Florence Griffith Joyner, the star of the Seoul [1988 Summer Olympics] was clean. Before 1988, her best times in the hundred metres and two hundred metres were, respectively, 10.96 and 21.96. In 1988, a suddenly huskier FloJo ran 10.49 and 21.34, times that no runner since has even come close to equalling. In other words . . . Griffith Joyner transformed herself in one season from a career-long better-than-average sprinter to the fastest female sprinter in history.[1]

Weather, not drugs, however, may have been a primary reason for Griffith Joyner's records, as her times were wind-assisted. Griffith Joyner retired from competition after the Seoul Olympics. She was only 38 years old when she died in 1998, the result of a severe epileptic seizure—not from the effects of any performance-enhancing drugs she may have used.

The Extent of Performance-Enhancing Drug Use

The specific number of professional or elite amateur athletes who use steroids or other performance-enhancing drugs is unknown, because athletes are not constantly tested for drug use and many of them are able to purchase drugs that are undetectable in tests. The results of drug tests do give some idea of the scope of the problem, however. Since 1989, 55 players in the National Football League have tested positive for performance-enhancing drugs. Slightly more than 11,000 athletes competed at the 2004 Summer Olympics in Athens, Greece. Twenty-four athletes failed drug tests either during or shortly before the Olympics; in the latter case, they were barred from competing. Five of the athletes were stripped of their medals. Twelve major league baseball players were suspended during the 2005 season for testing positive for steroids.

Elite athletes are not the only people who take performance-enhancing drugs. Many Americans have used anabolic steroids at least once in their lives. According to the Substance Abuse and Mental Health Services Administration's National Household Survey on Drug Abuse, 0.5 percent of the American adult population (1,084,000 adults) had taken anabolic steroids. Among adults between the ages of 18 and 34, the proportion increases to 1 percent. According to the 2005 Monitoring the Future Study, an annual report on drug use among teenagers, 1.2 percent of 8th-grade boys had used steroids during the previous year, compared with 1.8 percent of 10th graders and 2.6 percent of high school seniors. The rate of steroid use among girls is considerably lower—0.9 percent of 8th graders, 0.7 percent of high school sophomores, and 0.4 percent of 12th graders.

> **0.5 percent of the American adult population (1,084,000 adults) had taken anabolic steroids.**

According to a study conducted in 2001 by the National Collegiate Athletic Association (NCAA), 1 percent of college athletes use anabolic steroids. This number has dropped sharply since 1989, when 5 percent of athletes took steroids. Three percent of male football players use steroids; in 1989, that figure was 10 percent. Additionally, 3 percent of college athletes use amphetamines; that number has remained constant since 1989.

Why Do Athletes Use Performance-Enhancing Drugs?

Athletes use performance-enhancing drugs for a number of reasons; the specific reason generally depends on the level at which the athlete performs. Professional athletes who take these substances hope if they hit more home runs or sack more quarterbacks, they will make more money and receive more lucrative endorsements. Olympic and top-tier amateur athletes want to succeed in order to gain corporate sponsorships. College athletes want to be drafted into the professional leagues, while the goal of high school athletes is college scholarships. The myriad reasons for taking performance-enhancing drugs make their use a difficult problem to tackle because society cannot respond to or understand the needs of every athlete.

Moreover, any revelation that a well-known sports figure has been using a banned substance often paradoxically gives some measure of acceptability to the practice among the athlete's young fans. Greg Schwab, testifying before a U.S. Senate subcommittee, stated, "When a professional athlete admits to using steroids, the message young athletes hear is not always the one that is intended. Young athletes often believe that steroid use by their role models gives them permission to use."[2]

> " The myriad reasons for taking performance-enhancing drugs make their use such a difficult problem to tackle. "

Tackling the Problem of Performance-Enhancing Drugs

Many recent studies point to an increase in the use of performance-enhancing drugs among athletes. Almost across the board, more athletes are experimenting with these drugs in order to advance their careers and reap the financial rewards of athletic success. Jon Saraceno, in an article for *USA Today* concerning the spate of performance-enhancing drug stories during the summer of 2006 writes, "Generally speaking, we are fast suspending the capacity for belief in our fellow man/woman in matters involving the swarm of globe-trotting druggies and pushers posing as athletic marvels and high-tech trainers."[3]

Sports fans and commentators are calling for athletic organizations to decrease the prevalence of performance-enhancing drugs, as each major sporting event seems to bring with it a story of someone testing positive for using banned substances. For example, there were a number of positive drug tests and drug-related scandals in the 2004 Summer Olympics, the 2006 Winter Olympics, and the 2006 Tour de France, in which winner Floyd Landis was found to have tested positive for an unusually high level of testosterone. Major League Baseball (MLB) launched a major investigation into steroid use in 1999; as of the summer of 2006, it was still being conducted. John Hoberman, author of several books on performance enhancement, states, "The avalanche of revelations is a powerful reminder that doping subcultures have flourished for decades under the noses of officials and journalists who should have known better, or chose to keep quiet."[4]

This young fan encourages baseball players not to use steroids. Twelve Major League Baseball players were suspended during the 2005 season after testing positive for steroids.

Baseball's Steroid Investigation

In 2005 former professional baseball player Jose Canseco published his autobiography, *Juiced*, in which he detailed his use of steroids and named other prominent players, including Mark McGwire, who he alleged also used steroids. Congress launched an investigation into Canseco's claims. During hearings held in March 2005, some of the biggest baseball players, among them McGwire, Sammy Sosa, and Rafael Palmeiro, testified about their knowledge of steroid use in Major League Baseball. McGwire, who once hit a then-record 70 home runs in one season, refused to answer questions as to whether he had used steroids. Palmeiro categorically denied using any performance-enhancing drugs, only to test positive for steroid use a few months after his testimony.

> **Performance-enhancing drug use is likely to be part of the sports world for the foreseeable future.**

A Never-Ending Problem

Performance-enhancing drug use is likely to be part of the sports world for the foreseeable future. Tests are becoming more sophisticated, but so too is the technology to create undetectable drugs or develop techniques that are beyond anything that can be tested. For example, athletes may one day be able to genetically engineer their bodies to become faster or stronger.

In *Compact Research: Performance-Enhancing Drugs*, the issues surrounding drug use in sports are evaluated. These issues include whether using performance-enhancing drugs can be considered cheating, if these drugs are dangerous, whether testing is effective, and if the sports world can prevent the use of performance-enhancing drugs. Although athletes have taken such drugs for thousands of years, the future may be quite different.

Is the Use of Performance-Enhancing Drugs Cheating?

> **Athletes chemically propelled to victory do not merely overvalue winning, they misunderstand why winning is properly valued.**

—George F. Will, "Steroids Scandal Is Damaging to Baseball," *Conservative Chronicle*, December 2005.

A lthough modern-day athletes have used performance-enhancing drugs for decades, it was not until the 1960s that the leaders of the international and professional sports communities began to view the use of these drugs as cheating. The general disgust toward steroids and other performance-enhancing drugs has been especially strong since the late 1980s, following the discovery that Canadian sprinter Ben Johnson's world-record-setting victory in the 100-meter race in the 1988 Summer Olympics was fueled by his use of the steroid stanozolol. Before then, explains John Hoberman, a professor at the University of Texas and the author of several books on sports, "[the] use of performance enhancing substances was not viewed as cheating. It was simply a way of life for athletes of the times." [5]

Athletes in the past did not deny their use of performance-enhancing drugs; for example, in the 1970s, Olympic weightlifters openly declared their use of steroids. Howard Bryant, in his book *Juicing the Game*, writes: "Drugs were part of the weightlifting world. . . . Gyms across America provided the conduits to information about which substances worked best and where illegal drugs could be obtained." [6] The International Olympics Committee instituted drug testing in 1968 for narcotics and amphetamines, but steroids were not added to the list until 1975.

Until then, Olympians were free to add muscle to their body through chemical means, and athletes with access to the best performance-enhancing drugs could continue to use them without fear of punishment.

Reasons for Using Performance-Enhancing Drugs

Athletes use performance-enhancing drugs for a variety of reasons. Steroids increase strength and reduce the time it takes to recover from injury. As a result, athletes who use them are able to push themselves harder and further than a clean athlete. Increased strength allows them to record more tackles, hit a ball farther, and grab more rebounds. Other drugs increase the red blood cell count, allowing the blood to carry more oxygen and thus enabling the athlete to run or bike over long distances without tiring.

Yet no matter what sport they play, athletes know that their salaries are dependent on their statistics. It is therefore not surprising that so many would choose to artificially enhance their talents with performance-enhancing drugs. Few baseball fans can remember who hit the most singles in any given year, but almost all of them know that Barry Bonds set the MLB single-season home-run record with 73 home runs in 2001. Olympic medalists are famous for life; the athlete who finishes in fourth place in the 100-meter dash is soon forgotten, even if he or she was only a few hundredths of a second behind the gold medalist.

> " Athletes know that their their salaries are dependent on their statistics . . . [It's] not surprising that so many would choose . . . [to] enhance their talents with performance-enhancing drugs. "

Changing Views Toward Performance-Enhancing Drugs

Prior to the 1980s the lack of testing, other than in the Olympic Games, gave tacit approval to performance-enhancing drugs. The stories of rampant drug use in various professional sports leagues reveal a lackadaisical response that created a culture of acceptance and led to more and more athletes experimenting with drugs because they knew they could use whatever substances they wished without suffering any consequences. For example, Major League Baseball did not ban steroids until 2003, and once it did so, the penalty for failing a drug test was only a 10-game suspension.

However, the indifference toward performance-enhancing drugs that marked the 1960s through the middle of the 1980s began to be replaced by greater concerns as people became more aware of the health effects of these substances. Although the National Football League started testing for steroids in 1987, followers of the game likely did not recognize the dangerous effects of steroids until Lyle Alzado, a fearsome defensive end best known for his years with the Los Angeles Raiders, revealed in 1991 that he had brain cancer; he died the following year. Bryant writes, "Though many team doctors in the NFL doubted Lyle Alzado's claim that there was a direct connection between his steroid use and his brain cancer, his death in 1991 served as a sobering reminder of the influence of steroids in their sport."[7]

People also began to consider the use of performance-enhancing drugs to be cheating, because athletes were using the drugs to enhance their abilities unnaturally. Such usage thus distorts the notion of a level playing field and misinterprets the importance of sports, many people argue. President George W. Bush has stated, "The use of performance-enhancing drugs . . . sends the wrong message . . . that there are shortcuts to accomplishment, and that performance is more important than character."[8] Syndicated political columnist George Will suggests that the power of sports is diluted when winning becomes dependent on chemistry and not hard work.

Claims That Performance-Enhancing Drugs Have Limited Effects

One of the counterarguments to the idea that steroids cause a significant increase in athletic ability is that athletes still rely heavily on their natural ability; most people, no matter how hard they try, will never become professional or Olympic athletes. While performance-enhancing drugs can improve endurance and strength and speed up recovery, they cannot make a curve ball easier to hit or take seconds off of a sprinter's

100-meter time. As radio talk show host Steve Yuhas explains, "Popping a pill or injecting yourself with steroids, although harmful to the individual in the long run, does not make a person more athletically talented than anyone else."[9]

Some people even argue that natural ability is as unfair an advantage as performance-enhancing drugs—perhaps even more so, because while the drugs are available to anyone, athletes cannot change the genes with which they were born. In fact, many people contend that the use of performance-enhancing drugs is simply a way to level the playing field. They argue that it is genetics, not drugs, that make a competition unfair; some people are simply better equipped to compete. One example is Finnish cross-country skier Eero Maentyranta, who won three gold medals in the 1964 Winter Olympics. Later tests revealed his blood naturally contained 40 to 50 percent more red blood cells than average. This gave him a significant advantage over his competitors because long-distance performance relies on delivery of oxygen to muscles, which is the job of red blood cells. His natural ability outmatched any benefit someone with an average level of red blood cells would receive from using drugs.

> " Many people contend that the use of performance-enhancing drugs is simply a way to level the playing field. "

Similarly, one theory states that European distance runners lag behind their African counterparts because African runners, such as those from Kenya and Ethiopia, can resist fatigue longer and go farther on the same amount of oxygen. Studies also show that Kenyan runners tend to have slimmer legs than European runners, which means they do not need as much energy to run. Examination of this subject can be difficult, as it can lead to controversial conclusions on racial differences; however, physical evidence does suggest that body types are not universal—after all, no one would deny that the average man is too short to succeed in the National Basketball Association. As Julian Savulescu, Bennett Foddy, and Megan Clayton argue, "Sport discriminates against the genetically unfit. Sport is the province of the genetic elite."[10]

At the same time, note people who disagree with that argument, performance-enhancing drugs can make a significant difference if taken by an elite athlete. If taking a steroid will enable a hitter to develop the arm strength needed to drive a baseball 15 feet farther, that could be the difference between a fly ball to the warning track and a home run. Using EPO might enable a world-class sprinter to shave enough time off his or her 100-meter dash to win an Olympic medal. Talent is essential for athletic success, but performance-enhancing drugs can provide a small but critical boost. At the topmost levels of sports, differences between athletic ability are minimal, save for a few exceptional athletes—the Michael Jordans and Wayne Gretzkys of the world.

Legalizing Performance-Enhancing Drugs

Some argue that the best way to even the playing field is by legalizing performance-enhancing drugs. Proponents of this view contend that legalization would eliminate any genetic advantages some athletes may possess. One writer even suggests that athletes who do not use steroids should be banned from competition. In the view of Sidney Gendin, "For all the money they have to lay out, fans are entitled to the best possible performances. Why, then, should they have to put up with the inferior performances of non-drug users?"[11]

> **Some argue that the best way to even the playing field is by legalizing performance-enhancing drugs.**

Legalizing drugs would bring with it a host of new complications. First, each major sports organization would have to decide which performance-enhancing drugs its athletes would be permitted to use. The drugs would have to be strictly regulated to ensure that they were not laced with banned substances. Athletes would need to be recompensed if they developed health problems as a result of using steroids or other drugs. Society would also need to decide whether performance-enhancing drugs should be legalized at the high school or college level. In addition, as Charles E. Yesalis, an expert on the history of drugs in sports, states, "Legalization of steroids in sport might lessen hypocrisy, but it would place an extremely heavy burden on individual athletes who then would be forced either to take drugs known to be harmful or compete at a disadvantage."[12]

Whether using performance-enhancing drugs is a type of cheating or merely a way for athletes to create level playing fields is a matter of perspective. What is clear is that use of these drugs leads to considerable controversy and pointed debate. And as long as athletes come from different social and economic backgrounds and are of different shapes and sizes, athletic competitions can never take place between true equals.

Is the Use of Performance-Enhancing Drugs Cheating?

66 **The use of performance-enhancing drugs . . . sends the wrong message—that there are shortcuts to accomplishment, and that performance is more important than character.** 99

—George W. Bush, State of the Union address, January 20, 2004.

Bush is the 43rd president of the United States.

66 **Legalisation of doping, we believe, would encourage more sensible, informed use of drugs in amateur sport.** 99

—Bengt Kayser, Alexandre Mauron, and Andy Miah, "Legalisation of Performance-Enhancing Drugs," *Lancet*, December 17, 2005.

Kayser and Mauron are professors of exercise physiology and bioethics, respectively, at the University of Geneva in Switzerland. Miah is a lecturer in media, bioethics, and cyberculture at the University of Paisley in Scotland.

* Editor's Note: While the definition of a primary source can be narrowly or broadly defined, for the purposes of Compact Research, a primary source consists of: 1) results of original research presented by an organization or researcher; 2) eyewitness accounts of events, personal experience, or work experience; 3) first-person editorials offering pundits' opinions; 4) government officials presenting political plans and/or policies; 5) representatives of organizations presenting testimony or policy.

66 **Sports are inherently unfair. Genes alone do not make you a winner, of course, but some people's genes give them a massive advantage.** 99

–Michael Le Page, "Only Drugs Can Stop the Sports Cheats," *New Scientist*, August 19, 2006.

Le Page is a writer for the magazine *New Scientist*.

66 **The cheaters improve their performance. The cheaters endanger their health. The cheaters put pressure on the non-cheaters to make the same choice.** 99

—Joan Vennochi, "Facing the Truth About Baseball and Steroids," *Boston Globe*, March 15, 2005.

Vennochi is a columnist for the *Boston Globe*.

66 **If you think that athletics are an expression of human culture—perhaps even a form of popular art—then [performance-enhancing drug use] matters a great deal.** 99

—Danny Duncan Collum, "I Am What I Yam," *Sojourners*, March 2005.

Collum teaches writing at Bust College in Holly Springs, Mississippi.

66 **The cheaters are ahead of the testers, as they always will be. There's too much money to be made by the participants, and there's too much ego.** 99

—Rick Morrissey, "Clean Sweep: Drugs All Around," *Chicago Tribune*, July 12, 2006.

Morrissey is a sports writer for the *Chicago Tribune*.

❝If safe performance enhancement drugs were permitted, there would be greater pressure to develop safe drugs. Drugs would tend to become safer.❞

—Julian Savulescu, Bennett Foddy, and Megan Clayton, "Why We Should Allow Performance Enhancing Drugs in Sport," *British Journal of Sports Medicine*, 2004, p. 668.

Savulescu holds the Uehiro Chair of Practical Ethics at the University of Oxford. Foddy and Clayton work at the Murdock Children's Research Institute in Melbourne, Australia.

❝If we did legalize drugs in sport, that would mark the end of any traditional ideals of sport and competition.❞

—Charles E. Yesalis and Virginia S. Cowart, *The Steroids Game*. Champaign, IL: Human Kinetics, 1998.

Yesalis is a professor of exercise and sport at Pennsylvania State University. Cowart is a medical writer specializing in sports medicine.

❝Any dazzling world record [in track] instantly raises the specter of cheating.❞

—Merrell Noden, "A Great Ugly Cloud," *Sports Illustrated*, September 7, 1998.

Noden is the author of *Home Run Heroes: Mark McGwire, Sammy Sosa, and a Season for the Ages.*

❝The overall home run rates have shown a steady rise over the past 30 years—a trend that began even before the introduction of steroids.❞

—Ken Rosenthal, "Even with Testing, Offenses Will Be Pumped Up," *Sporting News*, March 4, 2005.

Rosenthal is a senior writer for *Sporting News*.

Facts and Illustrations

Is the Use of Performance-Enhancing Drugs Cheating?

- Since 2005, Major League Baseball has suspended 127 players for performance-enhancing drugs, including 113 in the minor leagues.

- Barry Bonds, who is being investigated for perjury over a 2003 denial of steroid use, set the MLB record in 2001 with 73 home runs in a single season.

- Annually, 1 percent of all athletes tested for performance-enhancing drugs test positive.

- When the National Football League tested for steroids for the first time, in 1987, it found that 30 percent of its players were using them.

- Twenty-four athletes tested positive at or shortly before the 2004 Summer Olympics in Athens.

- A report released by the National Collegiate Athletic Association in July 2006 revealed a 50 percent reduction in the number of students who tested positive for steroids in the 2004–2005 school year, compared to 1999–2000.

- Amphetamines have been used since the 1936 Summer Olympics.

- Three percent of college athletes use amphetamines.

How Drugs Improve Athletic Performance

Stimulants
Caffeine
Amphetamines
Cocaine

Relaxants
Alcohol
Beta-blockers
Cannabinoids

Mask Drug Use
Diuretics
Epitestosterone
Plasma expanders
Secretion inhibitors

Reduce Weights
Diuretics

Improved Athletic Performance

Mask Pain
Narcotics
ACTH
Cortisone
Local anesthetics

Build Muscle/Bone
Anabolic steroids
Beta-2 agonists
hCG
LH
hGH
IGF-1
Insulin

Increase Oxygen Delivery
EPO
Blood doping
Artificial oxygen carriers

Source: How Stuff Works, "How Performance Enhancing Drugs Work," 2006. www.howstuffworks.com.

- Steroids that are commercially available in the United States include stanozolol, nandrolone, and oxandrolone.

Most Baseball Fans Consider Player Steroid Use a Problem

Which comes closest to your view of steroid use among Major League Baseball players: it is ruining the game; it is a serious problem, but it is not ruining the game; it is not a serious problem; or it has made the game better?

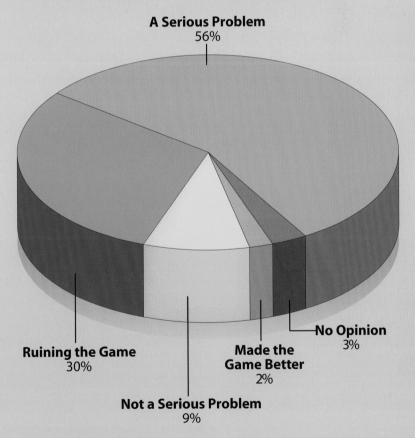

A Serious Problem
56%

Ruining the Game
30%

Made the Game Better
2%

No Opinion
3%

Not a Serious Problem
9%

According to a Gallup poll, a large majority of baseball fans think the game is adversely affected by player steroid use. Eighty-six percent feel that steroid use in Major League Baseball is a serious problem and/or ruining the game. Only 2 percent feel that steroid use improves the game.

Source: The Gallup Poll, 2005. www.gallup.com.

- Of Canadian school children, 2.8 percent have tested positive for steroids.

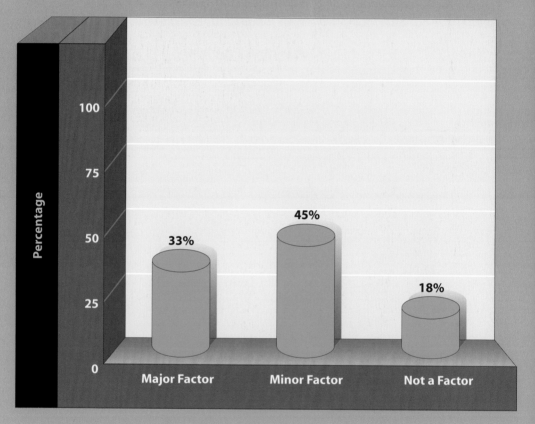

How Baseball Fans Think Player Steroid Use Impacts Game

Baseball fans: have steroids contributed to baseball's increased offensive output?

Critics of performance-enhancing drugs argue that their use creates an unfair advantage. According to a 2002 Gallup poll, 33 percent of baseball fans felt that steroid use in Major League Baseball significantly improved player performance. Conversely, 45 percent of fans said that steroid use was not a significant factor in player performance.

Source: The Gallup Poll, 2002. www.galluppoll.com.

How Professional Baseball Players Feel About Performance-Enhancing Drugs

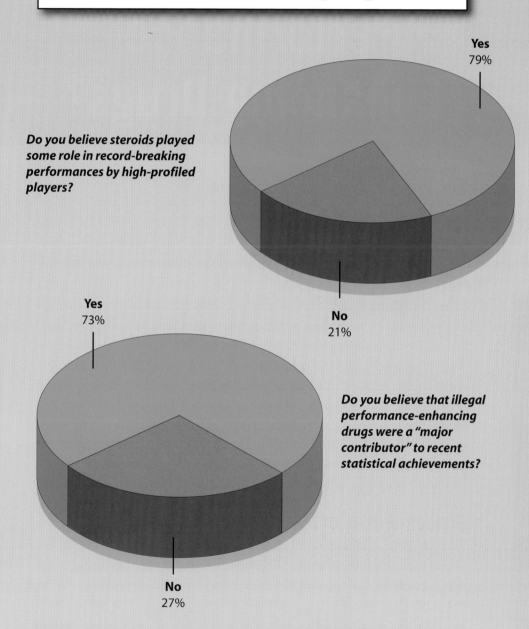

Do you believe steroids played some role in record-breaking performances by high-profiled players?

Yes 79%

No 21%

Yes 73%

No 27%

Do you believe that illegal performance-enhancing drugs were a "major contributor" to recent statistical achievements?

Source: *USA Today,* "Players Admit Steroids Changed Basball," 2005. www.usatoday.com.

31

How Dangerous Are Performance-Enhancing Drugs?

66 **The price of steroid abuse is high.** 99

—Doug West, "Steroid Abuse—Getting Bigger," *Youthculture@today*, Fall 2002.

Steroids and other performance-enhancing drugs do more than improve athletic performance. They can also shorten or worsen the lives of the athletes who use them. The physical effects of performance-enhancing drugs have been well documented. Steroid users run the risk of heart attacks, liver cancer, and strokes. Less fatal but still troubling consequences include impotence and breast development for male users and breast reduction and facial hair for women. These gender-specific effects occur because steroids contain testosterone; too much testosterone gives women male characteristics, but it also changes the secondary sexual characteristics of men. Excessive levels of testosterone have also been found to kill brain cells, a discovery that researchers believe may be linked to behavior changes such as suicidal tendencies and hyperaggressiveness.

Consequences of Steroid Use

The fate of East German women athletes who were given steroids to improve their chances in the Olympic games shows that using these drugs can have unintended consequences. Howard Bryant writes, "In thousands of cases, the East German government had injected so much testosterone into its female athletes that some had essentially turned into men. Breast size shrank, facial hair grew, male pattern baldness developed, and the clitoris grew enlarged and deformed. A few, their bodies ravaged by years' worth of male hormones, would undergo sex-change operations."[13]

Steroid users may also be more prone to injuries, in particular, tendon damage, because of their increased muscle mass. Some doctors believe this may be why Mark McGwire's home-run totals fell off rapidly after his record-setting season in 1998 and why injuries forced him to retire in 2001. Bryant suggests, "[Doctors] were . . . convinced that the types of injuries McGwire suffered were typical of a body affected by steroids, a by-product of overdevelopment, of joints weakened by anabolic substances, making his body far too powerful for his frame. McGwire grew so big his joints gave in."[14]

Steroids and Organ Damage

Steroids can cause serious harm to the heart, liver, and kidneys. People who use steroids have an increased chance of blood clots and of enlargement and weakening of the heart. Androgen use has also been associated with heart attacks. Because the liver filters blood before it reaches the kidneys, it must constantly work to remove traces of drugs, such as steroids, from the blood. If too large an amount of drugs reaches the liver, the organ releases bile into the bloodstream. Bile causes the eyes and skin to turn yellow, a condition known as jaundice. Steroid use can also result in liver tumors and the condition peliosis hepatitis, in which blood-filled cysts form in the liver. These can rupture and lead to internal bleeding. Extensive steroid use can also cause kidney failure because every drug a person takes also has to be processed through the kidneys.

> "Steroids can cause serious harm to the heart, liver, and kidneys."

Performance-enhancing drugs also affect athletes emotionally and psychologically. The hyperaggressiveness associated with steroid use is known colloquially as "'roid rage." Paranoia and antisocial behavior can also occur. Steroids can also be addictive, according to the Drug Enforcement Administration (DEA). The DEA explains, "An undetermined percentage of steroid abusers may become addicted to the drug, as evidenced by their continuing to take steroids in spite of physical problems, negative effects on social relations, or nervousness and irritability. Steroid users can experience withdrawal symptoms such as mood swings, fatigue, restlessness, and depression."[15]

The Side Effects of Human Growth Hormone and Blood Doping

Athletes may also experience serious physical problems when they take human growth hormone (HGH) or undergo blood doping. Side effects of HGH include heart problems, the enlargement of internal organs, and overgrown hands and feet. Athletes who return their own blood to their body via blood doping run the risk of blood clots, heart failure, and stroke. Using erythropoietin to mimic the effects of self-transfusion can increase the chances an athlete will suffer a stroke or heart attack because the increased red cell density caused by EPO thickens the blood, thereby forcing the heart to work harder to pump blood throughout the body.

Have the Dangers of Performance-Enhancing Drugs Been Exaggerated?

Despite these effects, many people maintain that performance-enhancing drugs are not terribly dangerous. One person who has argued that the health risks of steroid use have been overstated is Rick Collins, a bodybuilder and attorney who has written extensively about steroids. He asserts, "A flawed 1988 study suggested that psychiatric disorders occur with unusual frequency among athletes using anabolics. But the conclusions of these researchers have been regarded with skepticism from other experts."[16]

> " Some performance-enhancing drugs have legitimate medical uses and thus . . . should not be considered as wholly dangerous. "

Furthermore, some performance-enhancing drugs have legitimate medical uses and thus, proponents say, should not be considered as wholly dangerous. Steroids speed the healing of injured muscles, help aging men build muscle mass, and increase libido. Human growth hormone has helped increase the height of thousands of children.

Would Legalization Reduce the Health Risks of Performance-Enhancing Drugs?

Some contend that one way to make sure that athletes do not experience health problems when they take performance-enhancing drugs is to legalize these drugs. If steroids and similar substances were legalized, athletes could take them under the supervision of doctors. Michael Le Page, writing for *New Scientist*, argues, "Allow the use of drugs, and have sports authorities focus on testing the health of athletes rather than their use of drugs. This is the suggestion of ethicists Julian Savulescu at the University of Oxford and Bennett Foddy at the University of Melbourne, Australia. They argue that any drugs that are safe should be permitted, whatever their effect on performance." [17]

Le Page suggests that red blood cell concentration be monitored to ensure it does not reach dangerously high levels and that any athlete whose concentration exceeds that limit, for whatever reason, not be allowed to compete.

Le Page is not alone in his opinion. Writing for the medical journal *Lancet*, Bengt Kayser, Alexandre Mauron, and Andy Miah argue:

> If doping was allowed, would there be an increase in the rate of death and chronic illness among athletes? Would athletes have a shorter lifespan than the general population? Would there be more examples like the widespread use of performance-enhancing drugs in the former East-German republic? We do not think so. Only a small proportion of the population engages in elite sports. Furthermore, legalisation of doping, we believe, would encourage more sensible, informed use of drugs in amateur sport, leading to an overall decline in the rate of health problems associated with doping. [18]

Arguments Against Legalization

Legalization of performance-enhancing drugs is not an idea that has met with universal approval. Even if these drugs are legalized, opponents say, more potent versions are likely to be available on the black market. Athletes desperate to succeed may turn to the illegal versions and not receive necessary medical supervision. The international playing field may remain uneven if some nations approve of stronger steroids than do other nations. Additionally, athletes may ignore medical advice and continue to use performance-enhancing drugs even when they know their bodies may suffer permanent damage.

Legalization of these drugs also raises ethical concerns. Making performance-enhancing drugs legal might send a message to athletes that hard work is irrelevant and that it is more important to take shortcuts to success. This message could result in a rise in drug use among high school athletes, making it more difficult for coaches to teach lessons about fair play and hard work. Unscrupulous doctors might write prescriptions, even if they know doing so might cause harm to the athlete. Philippe Liotard, a professor at the University of Montpelier in France, writes of the dilemma facing doctors: "Doctors . . . who engage in [practices that allow athletes to compete despite injuries] are not performing their duty toward patients (which involves prescribing a halt to painful activity) but are complying with the demands of sport. From an ethical standpoint, a desired performance must not be taken into account in the course of diagnosis or treatment."[19]

> " Making performance-enhancing drugs legal might send a message to athletes that hard work is irrelevant and that it is more important to take shortcuts to success. "

Sports Are Inherently Dangerous

Many people contend that the physical and psychological consequences of performance-enhancing drugs are the least of an athlete's problems. They point out that athletics themselves are inherently unsafe, and injuries are common to every competition, from muscle strains in track and field to concussions in football and sometimes-fatal injuries in boxing. Some sports even revel in the brutality of the accidents, replaying bonecrushing hits and fiery race car crashes. Maxwell J. Mehlman, the director of the Law-Medicine Center at Case Western Reserve University School of Law, argues, "If athletes are free to accept a certain degree of risk from dangerous sports, why shouldn't they be allowed to accept a comparable, or even greater, risk from enhancements?"[20]

In response, others argue that even if athletes are prone to certain injuries, it does not necessarily follow that the use of substances that cause further problems should be encouraged. If steroids and other performance-enhancing drugs are as dangerous as they appear to be, then it is the responsibility of the sports community and society as a whole to find ways to reduce their use through testing and prevention efforts.

How Dangerous Are Performance-Enhancing Drugs?

66 **The evidence indicates that the feared downsides of steroid use, such as heart disease and prostate cancer, have been greatly overstated.** 99

—Patrick Cox, "Pumping Up Steroid Hysteria," Tech Central Station, February 11, 2004.   www.techcentralstation.com.

Cox is an economist and editorial columnist who has been published in the *Wall Street Journal* and *Reason* magazine.

66 **East German doping was very carefully regulated— and the results have been horrendous: several male athletes have developed cancerous breasts.** 99

—*Economist*, "Superhuman Heroes," June 6, 1998.

The *Economist* is a weekly magazine that covers world events and economics.

* Editor's Note: While the definition of a primary source can be narrowly or broadly defined, for the purposes of Compact Research, a primary source consists of: 1) results of original research presented by an organization or researcher; 2) eyewitness accounts of events, personal experience, or work experience; 3) first-person editorials offering pundits' opinions; 4) government officials presenting political plans and/or policies; 5) representatives of organizations presenting testimony or policy.

❝If athletes are free to accept a certain degree of risk from dangerous sport, why shouldn't they be allowed to accept a comparable, or even greater, risk from enhancements?❞

—Maxwell J. Mehlman, "Performance Enhancing Drugs in Sports," The Doctor Will See You Now. www.thedoctorwill seeyounow.com.

Mehlman is a professor of law and bioethics at Case Western Reserve University in Cleveland.

❝In a study of athletes, of the 53 current or past steroid users who underwent laboratory testing, only one subject displayed an abnormal liver test.❞

—Rick Collins, "Health Risks of Anabolic Steroids," SteroidLaw.com, 1999. www.steroidlaw.com.

Collins is a bodybuilder and criminal defense attorney who has defended clients involved with selling and using anabolic steroid products.

❝We cannot afford to jeopardize the health of our young people lured by the temptation of chemical shortcuts to greater athletic prowess.❞

—Joseph Rannazzisi, testimony before the House Subcommittee on Crime, Terrorism, and Homeland Security, March 16, 2004.

Rannazzisi is the deputy director of the Office of Diversion Control, which is part of the Drug Enforcement Administration.

❝I have always believed that dietary supplements can lead athletes to using performance-enhancing drugs like anabolic steroids.❞

—Greg Schwab, testimony before the U.S. Senate Subcommittee on Consumer Affairs, Foreign Commerce, and Tourism, June 18, 2002.

Schwab is the associate principal of Tigard High School in Tigard, Oregon.

> **❝More than half of boys ages 11 to 17 chose as their physical ideal an image possible to attain only by using steroids.❞**

—"Muscle Madness," March 2003. www.drugstory.org.

Drugstory.org is a Web site developed by the National Youth Anti-Drug media campaign in order to give up-to-date drug information to feature and entertainment writers.

> **❝Steroid users can experience withdrawal symptoms such as mood swings, fatigue, restlessness, and depression.❞**

—Drug Enforcement Administration, *Steroid Abuse in Today's Society*, March 2004.

The DEA enforces U.S. laws on illegal drugs.

> **❝[A steroid] is a drug that when it affects your body, you don't know if it is going to affect you now, 6 months down the road, or 10 years down the road.❞**

—Robert Hazelton, testimony before the House Subcommittee on Crime, Terrorism, and Homeland Security, March 16, 2004.

Hazelton is a former boxer who had to have both of his legs amputated because of damage caused by steroid use.

> **❝Strictly speaking, the assertion that any steroid use harms the user is not scientifically, soundly proven because the medical evidence is mixed.❞**

—Angela J. Schneider and Robert B. Butcher, "An Ethical Analysis of Drug Testing," in Wayne Wilson and Edward Derse, eds., *Doping in Elite Sport*, Champaign, IL: Human Kinetics, 2001, p. 136.

Schneider and Butcher are professors at the University of Western Ontario.

How Dangerous Are Performance-Enhancing Drugs?

- According to the 2005 Monitoring the Future survey, 57 percent of high school students believe that using steroids even once or twice is risky.

- A study of 227 men receiving treatment for opioid addiction found that 9.3 percent abused anabolic steroids before using any other illegal drugs.

- Use of performance-enhancing drugs can lead to heightened levels of aggression, a condition known as "'roid rage."

- The death of 26-year-old heptathlete Birgit Dressel on April 10, 1987, was caused by steroids, as the performance-enhancing drugs she used to rise in the world rankings led to a breakdown of her body's resistance.

- Between 500 and 2,000 former East German athletes are experiencing significant health problems associated with steroids, including liver tumors, heart disease, and testicular and breast cancer.

- Stimulants, which are used by athletes to stay alert, can cause hallucinations, circulatory problems, and convulsions.

- Adolescents can severely stunt their growth if they use steroids before their bodies have finished growing.

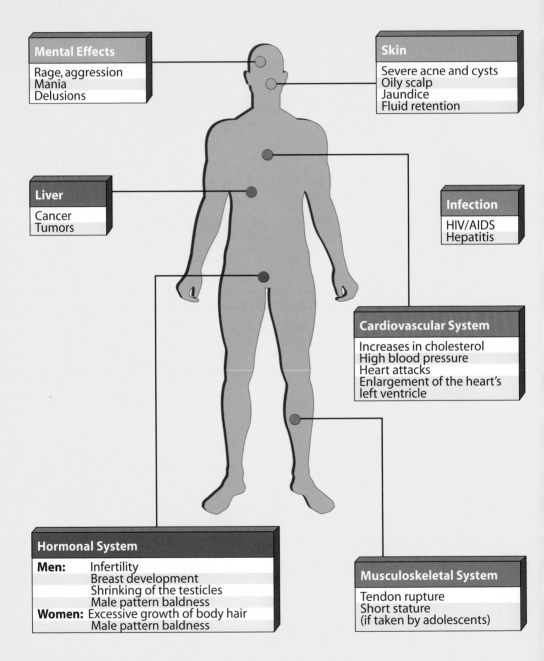

Potential Health Consequences of Anabolic Steroid Use

Mental Effects
Rage, aggression
Mania
Delusions

Skin
Severe acne and cysts
Oily scalp
Jaundice
Fluid retention

Liver
Cancer
Tumors

Infection
HIV/AIDS
Hepatitis

Cardiovascular System
Increases in cholesterol
High blood pressure
Heart attacks
Enlargement of the heart's
left ventricle

Hormonal System
Men: Infertility
Breast development
Shrinking of the testicles
Male pattern baldness
Women: Excessive growth of body hair
Male pattern baldness

Musculoskeletal System
Tendon rupture
Short stature
(if taken by adolescents)

Source: National Institute on Drug Abuse, research report, August 2006.

- British cyclist Tommy Simpson died while competing in the Tour de France cycling race in 1967. An autopsy revealed traces of amphetamines in his body.

- Former pro football player Lyle Alzado, who died of brain cancer, believed that steroid use caused his illness.

12th Graders' Perceived Harmfulness of Steroid Use

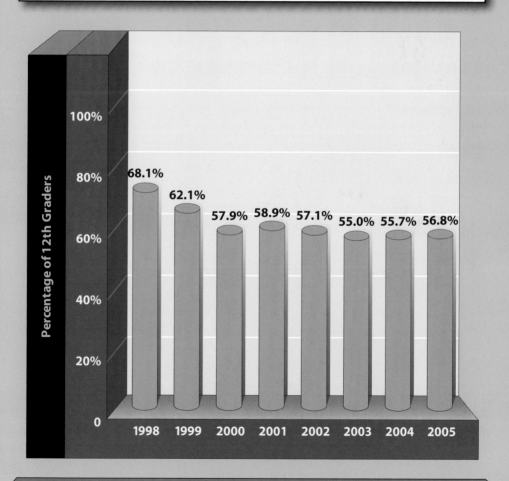

The results of this 2005 survey show that the number of high school seniors who view steroids as harmful has dropped significantly from 1998 to 2003; however, from 2003 to 2005, the number has slightly increased.

Source: Monitoring the Future survey, 2005.

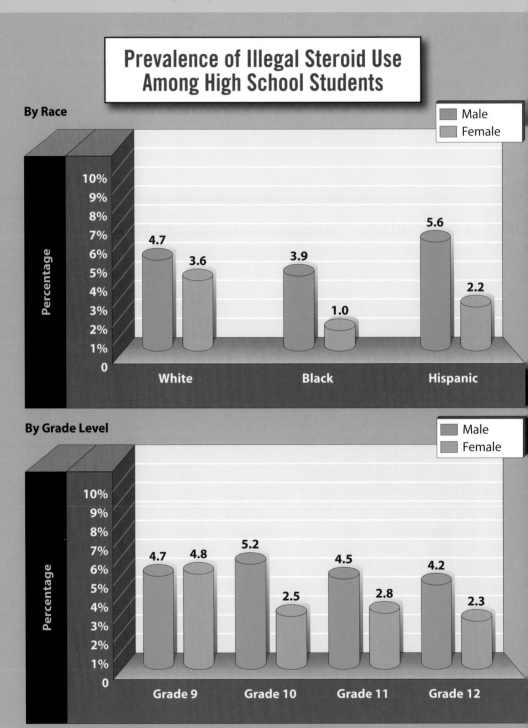

Prevalence of Illegal Steroid Use Among High School Students

By Race

Male
Female

Percentage

White — Male 4.7, Female 3.6
Black — Male 3.9, Female 1.0
Hispanic — Male 5.6, Female 2.2

By Grade Level

Male
Female

Percentage

Grade 9 — Male 4.7, Female 4.8
Grade 10 — Male 5.2, Female 2.5
Grade 11 — Male 4.5, Female 2.8
Grade 12 — Male 4.2, Female 2.3

The results of this 2005 survey indicate that illegal steroid use by high school students is higher among whites and Hispanics than blacks. Although, overall, males are more likely than females to use steroids, female 9th grade students have a slightly higher use rate than 9th grade males.

Source: Centers for Disease Control, *Morbidity and Mortality Weekly Report*, June 9, 2006.

- The average teenage girl produces 0.5 milligrams of testosterone each day. By contrast, girls competing in sports in Communnist East Germany received daily doses of 35 milligrams.

- Athletes who use EPO have an increased likelihood of suffering a stroke.

- People who inject steroids with contaminated needles are at risk of acquiring needle-borne diseases such as hepatitis or HIV.

- The overuse of human growth hormone can lead to disfigurement.

How Effective Is Testing for Performance-Enhancing Drugs?

> **" Policies tailor-formed by each league are at a risk of being overwhelmed by newer, more sophisticated threats, like . . . creative drug masking techniques. "**
>
> —Cliff Stearns, statement before the House Subcommittee on Commerce, Trade, and Consumer Protection, May 18–19, 2005.

Testing professional and amateur athletes for performance-enhancing drugs has become commonplace. Many prominent athletes, including world-class sprinters and cyclists, have been found guilty of using banned substances and subsequently were prohibited from playing or were suspended by their athletic federations. Questions have arisen, however, as to whether testing is effective or if it is a flawed system that can unfairly damage the reputations of athletes.

The Origins of Drug Tests

Tests that could detect banned substances were developed in the 1960s. In 1963, the International Olympic Committee (IOC) published its first list of banned substances. Random drug testing was initiated at the 1968 Winter Olympic Games; however, this initial effort was viewed mostly as an experiment by the IOC. A structured drug-testing effort was in place by the 1972 Summer Olympics in Munich, although testing for steroids was not possible until the next Olympics. Of the 275 samples tested at the 1976 Olympics in Montreal, 8 athletes tested positive. The National Basketball Association started to test its players for drug use in 1983. The National Football League began testing in 1987, but did not begin sanctioning players who failed a test until 1989. Major League Baseball started administering tests in 2003.

Testing for these drugs is typically accomplished in one of three ways: gas chromatography, mass spectrometry, or immuno-assays. The first two methods are used to test both urine and blood samples. Immuno-assays are biochemical tests that measure the levels of substances in urine. Athletes may be tested randomly throughout a season, at specific times, or immediately after competition, as is done in the Olympics.

Penalties for Positive Tests

Depending on the league or organization in which they compete, athletes experience different consequences if they test positive for performance-enhancing drugs. At the college level, any player who tests positive cannot compete for a full calendar year and also loses one year of athletic eligibility. The penalty for amateur track and field athletes depends on whether they test positive for stimulants or for anabolic steroids, certain amphetamines, or illegal doping techniques. In the case of stimulants, the penalty for a first offense is a public warning, disqualification from the event where the sample was taken, and the loss of any prize money or award from that event. A second positive test results in 2 years of ineligibility, and a third test leads to a lifetime ban. If the athlete is found to have used one of the other performance-enhancing drugs, he or she will be ineligible for 2 years after the first positive test and banned for life after a second positive test. The consequences for failing a drug test for cyclists is also harsh—a 2-year suspension after one offense.

> **Depending on the league or organization in which they compete, athletes experience different consequences if they test positive for performance-enhancing drugs.**

By contrast, the major professional sports leagues suspend their players for considerably shorter periods of time; however, because players are not paid during the length of their suspension, they do face a significant financial loss. Major League Baseball players face a 50-game suspension for a first positive test, 100 games for a second offense, and a season-long ban for a third offense. NFL players are suspended for 4 games for an initial offense and 8 games for a second positive test. Three positives lead to a 1-year suspension. Players in the National Hockey League receive a 20-game suspension for a first offense, a 60-game suspension for a second positive drug test, and a lifetime ban should they test positive for a performance-enhancing drug for the third time. Finally, the penalties for NBA players for a first, second, and third offense are as follows: 10 games, 25 games, and dismissal from the league, respectively.

The Effectiveness of Testing

Many people argue that drug testing has been effective. The National Collegiate Athletic Association and the major professional sports leagues have both asserted that the decline in steroid use among their athletes shows that tests have discouraged the use of performance-enhancing drugs. Jack L. Copeland, writing for *NCAA News* about the NCAA's drug-testing program, which was established in 1986, contends: "Doubts about the program's ability to effectively deter substance abuse have been satisfied."[21] Baseball commissioner Bud Selig has testified: "The positive rate for performance-enhancing substances in the 2003 testing was in the range of 5–7 percent. This disturbing rate triggered a more rigorous disciplinary testing program in 2004. This more effective program resulted in a decline of the positive rate to 1–2 percent."[22]

> " Infrequent tests allow high school students to use steroids during the summer. "

These statements, however, ignore the fact that drug testing is still often ineffective. High schools, for example, are rarely able to test student athletes for drugs because an individual test costs $175. Infrequent tests allow high school students to use steroids during the summer, increase their weight training during that time, then stop in enough time for the evidence of the drugs to pass out of their bodies before the athletes are tested in the fall. Taking drugs in cycles (using a substance for a few weeks, stopping for a period of time, and then resuming) also enables athletes to pass drug tests.

Athletes use other methods to pass drug tests as well. These tactics include the use of diuretics, which increase the volume of urine and thus make banned substances harder to detect, and renal blocking agents, which prevent steroids from entering the urine (and thus being detected). Athletes can also flirt with the edges of acceptable performance-enhancing drug use, especially where testing for erythropoietin is concerned. Malcolm Gladwell, in an article for the *New Yorker* magazine, writes that between 38 and 44 percent of the blood volume of the average adult male is red blood cells. Consequently, the International Cycling Union ruled that any rider whose percentage of red blood cells (their hematocrit) was above 50 percent would be suspended, to allow for riders with naturally high levels. As Gladwell writes, however, "The hematocrit standard had a perverse effect: it set the legal limit so high that it actually encouraged cyclists to titrate their drug use up to the legal limit." [23] Sports columnist Ken Rosenthal argues that professional baseball players can pass tests by taking lower doses of steroids—enough to reap the benefits, but not so much that they can be detected.

Drugs Are Outpacing Testing

Another factor that limits the effectiveness of testing is the fact that new variants of performance-enhancing drugs are being developed that cannot be detected by current tests. The steroid THG, for example, was discovered only after a coach sent a sample vial of the drug to the World Anti-Doping Agency. The drug was traced to the Bay Area Laboratory Cooperative, better known as BALCO. Moreover, no one test can detect all illegal substances. For example, human growth hormone can be detected only in blood tests, yet most sports organizations test only urine.

Unintentional Cheating

Still another limitation of drug tests is that athletes can fail not because they intend to cheat but because they made an unintentional mistake. For example, an athlete who is suffering from a cold may take a medicine that contains pseudoephedrine, a banned substance. Baseball players who live in Latin America during the off season can legally purchase steroids there and may not realize that steroids are illegal in the United States. Athletes might also ingest dietary supplements whose contents are not accurately labeled and thus take steroids without having intended to do so.

Testing Does Not Change the Past

Testing can also be ineffective because it cannot be used to penalize athletes who used formerly legal substances to set new records. Sports commentators criticized baseball slugger Mark McGwire when he acknowledged using androstenedione during the 1998 season, when he hit 70 home runs; however, baseball had not banned the substance at that time. Barry Bonds may have used steroids when he hit 73 home runs in 1 season, but baseball did not ban their use for another 2 years. Testing cannot be ex post facto; it can be used only to help prevent similar events from occurring in the future. For Olympic athletes who were cheated out of a medal because other competitors broke the rules, however, that may be of little comfort.

Athletes Are Presumed Guilty

Concerns about drug testing go beyond whether it is effective. A major drawback surrounding drug tests is the pervasive attitude in sports today that an athlete is guilty until proven innocent. One fact that many sports fans do not realize is that performance-enhancing drug use cannot be proved definitively unless two samples provided by an athlete (from the same urine specimen) are found to contain those drugs. On a number of occasions an athlete has been reported guilty of using steroids, only to have a second test prove otherwise. This situation befell track and field star Marion Jones in 2006—she initially tested positive for EPO at the USA Track and Field Championships, but was later cleared. Drug tests are also imperfect. Immunoassays give false positive results approximately 5 percent of the time.

> A major drawback surrounding drug tests is the pervasive attitude in sports today that an athlete is guilty until proven innocent.

Sometimes athletes are believed to have used performance-enhancing drugs because they associate with other athletes or coaches known to use or condone such tactics. One reason that people were more inclined to believe that Marion Jones was guilty of using EPO and other performance-enhancing drugs was the various men with whom she had associated. Jones's former husband, shot-putter C.J. Hunter, was suspended in 2001 for 2 years because nandrolone was found in his system. Two of Jones's former coaches, Charlie Francis and Trevor Graham, have been connected with athletes who have used these drugs; Francis coached Ben Johnson. Lastly, Tim Montgomery, with whom Jones had a child, was banned from competition for 2 years after being charged with using illegal performance-enhancing drugs.

> **A positive drug test can be nearly impossible for an athlete to overcome.**

Similarly, the success of Irish swimmer Michelle Smith at the 1996 Summer Olympics, where she won 3 gold medals, raised suspicions because her husband/coach had once been banned for 4 years for using illegal drugs during his discus-throwing career. In fact, Smith (whose married name was Michelle de Bruin) was later banned for 4 years because a urine sample she submitted for a 1998 test had been altered—its alcohol content was suspiciously high. Such situations are not limited to the Olympics. A host of professional athletes, including baseball star Bonds, are believed to have used performance-enhancing drugs because of information found in the BALCO investigation. One of those figures, baseball player Jason Giambi, has admitted to steroid use.

A positive drug test can be nearly impossible for an athlete to overcome. Floyd Landis's dramatic victory in the 2006 Tour de France was sullied after he failed a drug test on a day when he engineered one of the greatest comebacks in cycling history. He was subsequently dismissed by his cycling team, Phonak. Landis has maintained his innocence, arguing that his body naturally produces a high amount of testosterone and that thyroid medication may also have affected the results. It was discovered in November 2006 that one of his samples was misrecorded by the French laboratory that conducted the tests. Such a discovery raises questions as to the validity of the tests, but the damage done to Landis's reputation cannot be recovered if he is eventually proven innocent.

An Imperfect System

Testing for performance-enhancing drugs is not perfect; however, despite the inability of drug tests to catch every instance of cheating, statistics do suggest that the growth in testing since the 1980s has led to a decline in use among athletes. Whether testing technology can ever catch up with the scientific advances available to elite athletes is a question that remains to be answered.

Primary Source Quotes*

How Effective Is Testing for Performance-Enhancing Drugs?

66 Antidoping regulations are an integral part of the 'rules of the game,' similar to those regulating playing equipment, scoring competition results, and penalizing infractions. 99

—Matthew J. Mitten, "Is Drug Testing of Athletes Necessary?" *USA Today* magazine, November 2005.

Mitten is the director of the National Sports Law Institute and a professor at Marquette University Law School.

66 The present system of doping control too often violates the rights of athletes. 99

—David L. Black, "Doping Control Testing Policies and Procedures: A Critique," in Wayne Wilson and Edward Derse, eds., *Doping in Elite Sport.* Champaign, IL: Human Kinetics, 2001.

Black is the chairman and president of Aegis Sciences Corporation, a company that assists sports organizations with drug testing.

* Editor's Note: While the definition of a primary source can be narrowly or broadly defined, for the purposes of Compact Research, a primary source consists of: 1) results of original research presented by an organization or researcher; 2) eyewitness accounts of events, personal experience, or work experience; 3) first-person editorials offering pundits' opinions; 4) government officials presenting political plans and/or policies; 5) representatives of organizations presenting testimony or policy.

❝I believe what fans want is some assurance that steroid use in baseball is eliminated and this system should be given a chance.❞

—Jody Gerut, "Steroids: A Player's Perspective," March 25, 2004. www.cleveland.com.

Gerut is a Major League Baseball player who has played for the Cleveland Indians, Chicago Cubs, and Pittsburgh Pirates.

❝Tougher testing won't reverse the increase in [baseball] offense. The best it can do is make things more normal again.❞

—Ken Rosenthal, "Even with Testing Offenses Will Be Pumped Up," *Sporting News*, March 4, 2005.

Rosenthal is a columnist for *Sporting News*.

❝Athletes with access to the right resources can beat the drug tests. Other athletes can not [*sic*].❞

—Anonymous, "The History of Drug Testing in Sports and How Athletes Beat the Drug Tests," MESO-Rx.com, 2002. www.meso-rx.com.

The anonymous author was involved with drug testing for various sports.

❝The 2002 [MLB drug testing] agreement that has been roundly criticized in some circles actually resulted in a significant reduction in steroid use.❞

—Bud Selig, statement before the U.S. House Committee on Government Reform, March 17, 2005.

Selig is the commissioner of Major League Baseball.

> **It is clear that the NCAA has a [drug-testing] program that was well-planned and legally sound, but retains the flexibility to change with the times.**

—Jack L. Copeland, "Drug Testing Program Withstanding the Test of Time," *NCAA News*, September 30, 2002.

Copeland is a writer for the *NCAA News*, a publication of the National Collegiate Athletic Association.

> **Performance-enhancing drugs have not been an issue in the NHL.**

—Gary Bettman, statement before the House Subcommittee on Commerce, Trade, and Consumer Protection, May 18–19, 2005.

Bettman is the commissioner of the National Hockey League.

> **Maybe the NFL hasn't solved this potentially deadly problem [of steroids]. . . . But give league management and the players a lot of credit for trying.**

—Nick Cafardo, "NFL's Steroid Program Has Been a Major Success," *Boston Globe*, June 13, 2002.

Cafardo is a reporter for the *Boston Globe*.

> **Some athletes may be innocently tainted, but that's the only way to target the far greater number of cheats.**

—Mark Starr, "One Strike, You're Out," *Newsweek*, November 8, 2001.

Starr is a sports columnist for *Newsweek* magazine.

❝I used to think [Marion] Jones' 10-year record of accomplishments on the track made her immune from suspicion. . . . I now see that I was wrong.❞

—Ron Rapoport, "Games Put to Test," *Chicago Sun-Times*, September 6, 2000.

Rapoport is a writer for the *Chicago Sun-Times*, a daily newspaper.

How Effective Is Testing for Performance-Enhancing Drugs?

- Only 13 percent of U.S. high schools have a drug testing program.

- In 2002 the National Collegiate Athletic Association spent $3 million on drug testing.

- Fifty-five percent of college athletes, according to a survey conducted by the National Collegiate Athletic Association, believe that drug testing deters drug use.

- Drug tests cost $175 each.

- The National Basketball Association conducts more than 9,000 drug tests each season.

- During the preseason and regular season, the National Football League conducts more than 9,000 tests for steroids and other banned substances.

- According to the International Amateur Athletic Federation, only 10 to 15 percent of athletes are tested at major competitions.

- More than 40 Chinese swimmers have tested positive for steroids since 1990.

- Forty-seven professional tennis players have tested positive for the banned steroid nandrolone.

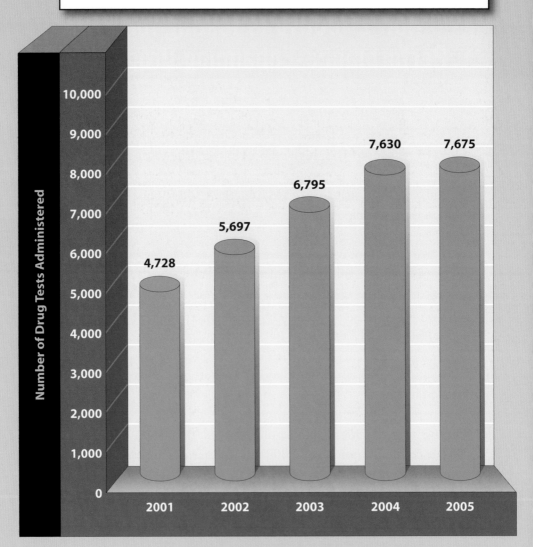

U.S. Anti-Doping Agency Testing, 2001–2005

Number of Drug Tests Administered

Year	Tests
2001	4,728
2002	5,697
2003	6,795
2004	7,630
2005	7,675

The U.S. Anti-Doping Agency is responsible for testing U.S. Olympic athletes for performance-enhancing drug use. This chart shows a significant increase in testing from 2001 to 2005.

Source: United States Anti-Doping Agency, "Annual Testing," 2006. www.usantidoping.org.

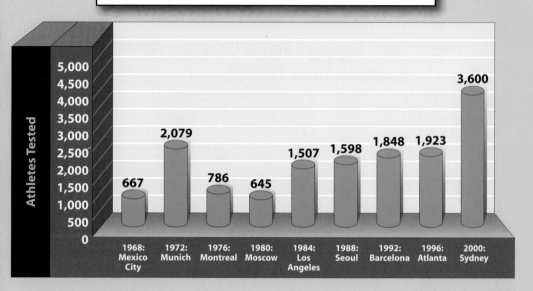

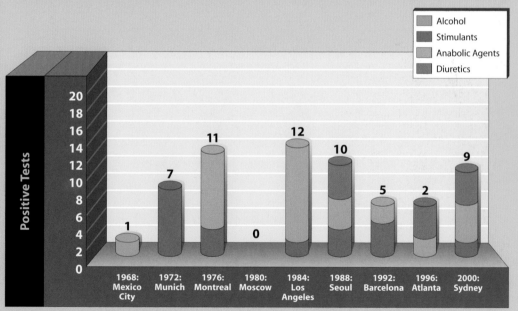

The International Olympic Committee has been testing Olympic athletes since 1967. In that time, the number of athletes tested has generally increased, and most positive tests indicated anabolic agents such as steroids. Stimulants, such as amphetamines, were the next most common type of drug indicated in positive tests.

Source: International Olympic Committee.

- Injected steroids can be detected in the body for 3 to 4 months, while oral steroids remain detectable for 1 to 4 weeks.

Most Fans Support Major League Baseball Drug Testing

Should Major League Baseball players be tested for performance-enhancing drugs?

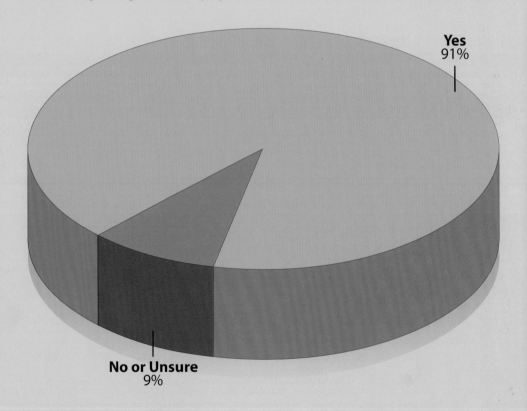

Yes
91%

No or Unsure
9%

In a 2004 Gallup poll of baseball fans, 91 percent supported drug testing of Major League Baseball players. Amid controversy, Major League Baseball and the Players Association agreed in late 2005 to a new, far more stringent testing policy for steroids and stimulants like amphetamines.

Source: *USA Today*/Gallup/CNN Poll, 2004.

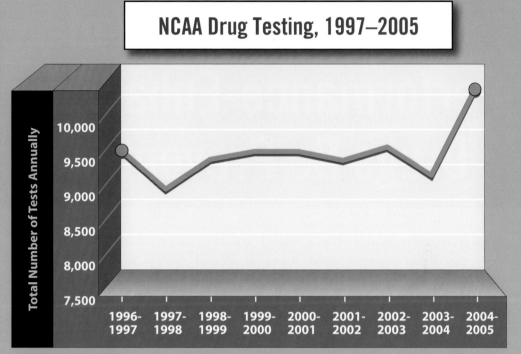

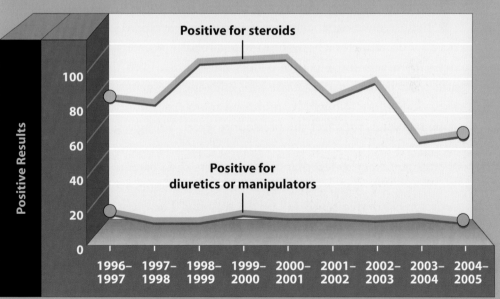

This drug testing information comes from the National Collegiate Athletic Association Drug-Testing Program, which is committed to protecting the health of college athletes and ensuring that no artificial advantage exists in collegiate sports. Over the eight-year period, those testing positive for steroids and diuretics (masking agents) both dropped.

Source: NCAA "Year-Round Test Results Summary," July 6, 2006.

61

How Can the Use of Performance-Enhancing Drugs Be Prevented?

> **"Athletes and others must understand that they can excel in sports and have a great body without steroids."**
>
> —Drug Enforcement Administration, *Steroid Abuse in Today's Society,* March 2004.

The culture of athletics has made creating effective prevention programs a challenge. Athletes at all levels have come to feel that using performance-enhancing drugs is not only accepted but is in fact a necessity for athletes who want to win scholarships or sign multimillion-dollar contracts and lucrative endorsement deals. Even the youngest of athletes believe that they must win; enjoying the game and improving their skills is not enough. As more and more expectations are placed on young athletes, they feel the pressure to excel. Young athletes recognize that their parents are more appreciative of them when they play well, and they do not want to feel that they are letting their parents down.

When the main goal in sport is to win, issues of fair play and sportsmanship frequently fall by the wayside. The question of whether or not the use of performance-enhancing drugs is cheating becomes moot because athletes feel that it is acceptable to win at any cost. U.S. sprinter Kelli White, in testimony before Congress, stated that she had been willing to use a variety of banned substances, including the designer steroid THG, because she was struggling to succeed in international competition. Her efforts to improve her athletic standing were doomed, however, because she failed a drug test and was banned from competition for two years.

Athletes are even willing to sacrifice their lives in exchange for success. Since 1982, Dr. Bob Goldman, an osteopath, has asked 200 athletes the same two questions each year. The first question is, "You are offered a banned performance-enhancing substance, with two guarantees: 1) You will not be caught. 2) You will win. Would you take the substance?" All but one or two of the athletes usually say "yes." He next asks, "You are offered a banned performance-enhancing substance, with two guarantees: 1) You will not be caught. 2) You will win every competition you enter for the next five years, and then you will die from the side effects of the substance. Would you take the substance?"[24] Each year, despite knowing the deadly consequence of the performance-enhancing drug, more than half the athletes questioned say yes.

> **43 percent of American adults believe that at least half of the professional athletes in the United States use steroids.**

Sports fans, disappointed by repeated stories of failed drug tests, such as the spate of positive tests that marred the 1998 Tour de France, are likely to think poorly of athletes, even those who would not take Goldman's offer. Only 6 percent of the adults surveyed by Harris Interactive said that no professional baseball players use steroids or other performance-enhancing drugs. According to a poll conducted by the *New York Times*, 43 percent of American adults believe that at least half of the professional athletes in the United States use steroids.

Toughening Penalties for Performance-Enhancing Drug Use

Preventing performance-enhancing drug use is difficult because testing has often been ineffective, and the punishment for getting caught, until recently, was relatively minor. If athletes feel that the penalties cause little more than a disruption of their season, it is less likely that they will worry about possibly failing a drug test. In the National Football League, a first-time offender is suspended for 4 games, or 25 percent of the regular season. Major League Baseball initially established a policy that would require a first-time offender to receive treatment, and a second positive steroid test would lead to a 15-day suspension. In 2005 the MLB increased the consequences of a positive test. A first positive test would result in a 10-game suspension. A second test would lead to a 30-game suspension, 3 positives would cause the player to be suspended for 60 games, 4 positives would lead to a 1-year suspension, and a player who tested positive for steroids 5 times would be penalized at the commissioner's discretion. All players would be tested at least once each year.

Baseball team owners and players approved even tougher penalties in November 2005. The first positive test would result in a 50-game suspension. If a player tested positive a second time, he would be suspended for 100 games. Any player testing positive for steroids 3 times would receive a lifetime suspension. Professional league suspensions cost the players monetarily, as they do not receive their salary while suspended and are not likely to receive commercial endorsements.

Drug Free Sports Act

The federal government has become involved in preventing the use of performance-enhancing drugs. Congress passed the Anabolic Steroid Control Act in 2004, which made it illegal for people to use androstenedione as a performance-enhancing drug. In 2005, Congress began debate on the Drug-Free Sports Act.

The act, which has yet to be put to a vote, would require professional athletes to be tested at least once per year and would suspend for two years athletes who fail drug tests.

Not everyone believes that the government has the right to decide what substances adult athletes can or cannot use. The heads of major sports, such as former NFL commissioner Paul Tagliabue, argue that attempts to develop uniform rules on drug testing are unfair and do not take into consideration the differences between the sports. He testified before Congress, "A uniform system for all sports will necessarily fail to account for the differences among sports organizations in structure, length of season, number of players, average career length, and program cost."[25] Donald Fehr, executive director of the MLB Players Association, notes that suspending a player for two years after the first positive drug test could end many careers. Such a concern is echoed by the NFL, where the average career is only four years long.

International Concerns

Even if the United States is one day able to end the problem of steroids in college sports and the four major sports leagues, performance-enhancing drugs may continue to be an international problem. Unless all countries make a concerted effort to ensure that their athletes compete cleanly, it is almost inevitable that some nations will continue to allow cheating. East Germany became notorious during the 1970s and 1980s for giving its Olympic athletes steroids, while Chinese swimmers were caught up in similar scandals in the 1990s. The United States is not problem-free either. Wade Exum, the former director of drug control administration for the U.S. Olympic Committee, acknowledged in 2003 that 19 American medalists who competed in the Olympic Games between 1988 and 2000 had done so despite failing drug tests. Reportedly, 1 of the athletes was track and field legend Carl Lewis.

> Unless all countries make a concerted effort to ensure that their athletes compete cleanly, it is almost inevitable that some nations will continue to allow cheating.

Furthermore, the international aspect of performance-enhancing drug use receives little attention most of the time, except during major events such as the Olympics, track and field world championships, and the Tour de France. A drug scandal at those times is covered in depth by the media but soon forgotten once the athletes have returned home. Constant awareness of the international sports scene is vital if performance-enhancing drugs are to be fought on a global basis.

Changing Attitudes Toward Drugs and Sports

Instead of trying to prevent the use of performance-enhancing drugs, some argue, perhaps society should change the way it views sports. In an article written for *Sports Illustrated*, Merrill Noden suggests, "Since human evolution can't keep pace with our hunger for new records, and neither can advances in training, why not reemphasize competition over records? Who can actually see the difference between a 9.84 100 and a

10.04 100? But a close race, with two or three athletes straining toward the finish, now that's exciting."[26]

Oliver Morton, writing for *Newsweek International*, suggests taking a different approach. In his view, two Olympics should be held, one for athletes who use drugs and one for those who do not. In this way, Morton argues, all athletes would have an equal opportunity to succeed and none would feel compelled to use performance-enhancing drugs.

The Role of Education in Preventing Steroid Use

In May 2005 the California Interscholastic Federation (CIF) put into place a three-part program to reduce steroid use. This program did not include mandatory testing but instead relied on a multipronged approach to create a culture in which a student athlete had both the information and the support to make sound decisions about steroid use.

> No program can stop athletes determined to cheat.

First, each athlete and his or her parents were required to express, in writing, that the student would not use steroids without a doctor's prescription. Second, all coaches were required to complete a coaching education certificate program that contained a section on performance-enhancing drugs. Lastly, anyone associated with the school was prohibited from selling or advocating performance-enhancing dietary supplements, even those that were legal. The efforts put forth by the CIF show that performance-enhancing drug education must be part of the student athlete's life; it cannot be limited to a lecture or a pamphlet.

Education is also an important facet of prevention programs in professional sports. For example, the antidrug program run by the National Basketball Association "has always had a strong emphasis on education and treatment instead of punishment,"[27] according to Antonio Davis, president of the National Basketball Players Association. He explained before a Senate committee that any NBA player who fails a drug test must enter an education, treatment, and counseling program. NBA players also attend yearly meetings on the dangers of performance-enhancing drugs. Major League Baseball has collaborated with the Partnership for a Drug-Free America to teach young athletes about the dangers of performance-enhancing drugs.

Using education rather than legislation is a tactic praised by Doug Bandow, a senior fellow at the Cato Institute. In an article criticizing Congress's efforts to fight steroid abuse, he writes, "[Steroids] are not good. But that hardly constitutes a national crisis. . . . There is a need for more parental involvement, improved educational efforts, and better rules enforcement."[28] According to Bandow, the responsibility for keeping children away from steroids belongs to parents and teachers, not politicians.

No Perfect Solution

The use of performance-enhancing drugs is an international problem that affects virtually every sport. Stricter laws and education may help prevent athletes from using illegal substances, but doubts will likely remain no matter what type of prevention program is instituted. No program can stop athletes who are determined to cheat or convince sports fans or commentators that the games they watch are won or lost solely on the basis of talent and hard work.

How Can the Use of Performance-Enhancing Drugs Be Prevented?

66 If you want to get rid of performance-enhancing drugs in team sports, start punishing the team owners, coaches, universities and high schools that financially benefit from steroid abuse. 99

—Jason Whitlock, "Steroid Users Victim of System," *Kansas City (MO) Star*, August 29, 2006.

Whitlock is a sports columnist for the *Kansas City Star*.

66 Performance-enhancing drugs may not be desirable, but they are here to stay. What we can do away with is the hypocrisy. 99

—Adrianne Blue, "Sports: It's the Real Dope," *New Statesman*, August 14, 2006.

Blue is an author and journalist who has written extensively on sports, including the books *Queen of the Track* and *Grace Under Pressure*.

66 It is far more important to preserve a free society than to stop athletes from making bad decisions. 99

—Doug Bandow, "Busy Bodies on Steroids," *American Spectator*, December 10, 2004.

Bandow is a senior fellow at the Cato Institute, a libertarian research organization.

* Editor's Note: While the definition of a primary source can be narrowly or broadly defined, for the purposes of Compact Research, a primary source consists of: 1) results of original research presented by an organization or researcher; 2) eyewitness accounts of events, personal experience, or work experience; 3) first-person editorials offering pundits' opinions; 4) government officials presenting political plans and/or policies; 5) representatives of organizations presenting testimony or policy.

❝The non-steroid user . . . manages to be competitive only because better athletes are unfairly being kept out of sports.❞

—Sidney Gendin, "Let's Ban Those Who Don't Use Drugs," MESO-Rx, Fall 2000. http://meso-rx.com.

Gendin is a professor emeritus of philosophy of law at Eastern Michigan University in Ypsilanti.

❝The current effectively unregulated availability of products containing steroid precursors in the United States is a health crisis.❞

—Ralph W. Hale, statement before the U.S. House Subcommittee on Crime, Terrorism, and Homeland Security, March 16, 2004.

Hale is the chairman of the board of directors of the United States Anti-Doping Agency.

❝High school sports are a proving ground for college. So kids feel like they need to impress everyone who is watching.❞

—Darian, "Foul Play: Sports, Doping and Teens." www.drugstory.org.

Darian is a Los Angeles–area high school athlete.

❝The fight against drugs in sports is an extremely difficult battle. I am sorry that I cheated myself, my competitors, my sport, my family and the public.❞

—Kelli White, testimony before the U.S. Senate Committee on Commerce, Science, and Transportation, May 24, 2005.

White is a former U.S. Olympic sprinter.

❝[The Drug Free Sports Act] would not improve upon the NFL's current program.❞

—Paul Tagliabue, testimony before the U.S. House Subcommittee on Commerce, Trade, and Consumer Protection, March 18–19, 2005.

Tagliabue is the former commissioner of the National Football League.

❝We believe the goal [of eliminating performance-enhancing drugs] is best accomplished by the leagues and players working together.❞

—Antonio Davis, testimony before the U.S. Senate Committee on Commerce, Science, and Transportation, September 28, 2005.

Davis is a professional basketball player and the president of the National Basketball Players Association. Teams he has played for include the Chicago Bulls and the Indianapolis Pacers.

❝Athletes who refuse drugs may eventually come to be seen as quaint anachronisms.❞

—Oliver Morton, "Coming Soon: Open Olympics!" *Newsweek International*, July 12, 1999.

Morton is a contributing editor at *Newsweek International*.

❝The most important aspect to curtailing abuse is education concerning dangerous and harmful side effects.❞

—Drug Enforcement Administration, "Anabolic Steroids," March 2004.

The DEA enforces the drug laws of the United States.

Facts and Illustrations

How Can the Use of Performance-Enhancing Drugs Be Prevented?

- According to a 2005 survey, 18.1 percent of 8th graders, 29.7 percent of 10th graders, and 39.7 percent of 12th graders reported that steroids were "fairly easy" or "very easy" to obtain.

- The International Olympics Committee has found that 41 percent of 624 dietary supplements used by Olympic athletes contain a steroid precursor or banned substance.

- The average National Basketball Association player would lose $450,000 if suspended for 10 games for a positive steroid test.

- A National Football League player who tests positive for steroids or another banned substance faces up to 24 unannounced tests during the following year.

- The Anabolic Steroid Control Act of 2004 classified androstenedione as a controlled substance and made its use as a performance-enhancing drug illegal.

- Ninety-four percent of American adults surveyed in a March 2004 poll said they believe approximately one-third of professional baseball players use performance-enhancing drugs.

- Members of Congress proposed the Drug Free Sports Act in 2005 as a way to institute uniform drug testing among the four major professional sports leagues. As of November 2006 the act had not become law.

- In 2002 the International Olympic Committee required all international sports bodies to adopt the World Anti-Doping Code.

Positive Tests of Performance-Enhancing Drugs Internationally

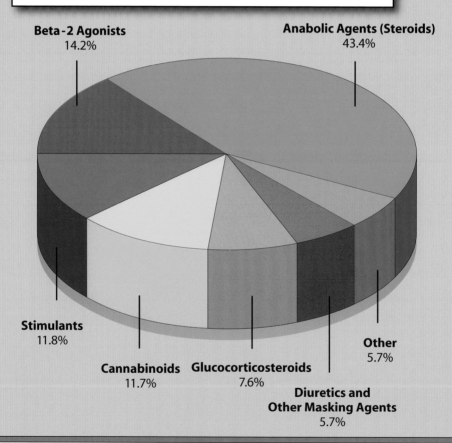

Beta-2 Agonists
14.2%

Anabolic Agents (Steroids)
43.4%

Stimulants
11.8%

Cannabinoids
11.7%

Glucocorticosteroids
7.6%

Other
5.7%

Diuretics and Other Masking Agents
5.7%

This chart illustrates the worldwide prevalence of specific types of drugs discovered through testing of Olympic and non-Olympic athletes. Of all reported positive tests, 43.4 percent indicated anabolic agents, including steroids.

Source: The World Anti-Doping Agency, 2005 Annual Report.

Positive Test Results for Performance-Enhancing Drugs Increasing

tal Number of Tests

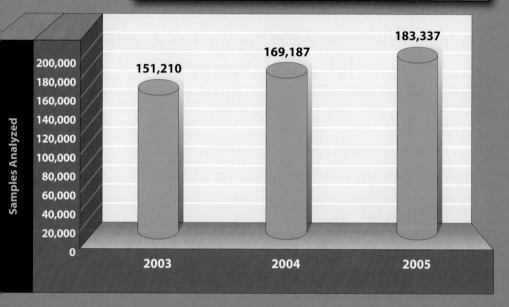

Samples Analyzed

- 151,210 (2003)
- 169,187 (2004)
- 183,337 (2005)

sitive Results

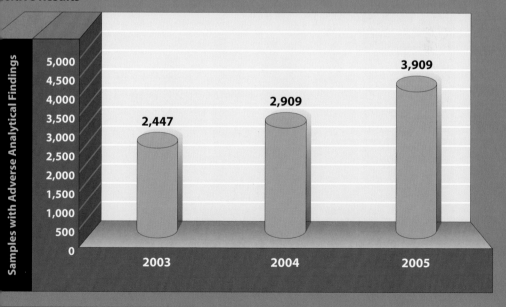

Samples with Adverse Analytical Findings

- 2,447 (2003)
- 2,909 (2004)
- 3,909 (2005)

These graphs show testing by countries around the world of Olympic and non-Olympic athletes from 2003 to 2005. While the total number of tests increased 21 percent, the number testing positive for performance-enhancing drugs increased 60 percent.

rce: World Anti-Doping Agency, 2005 Annual Report.

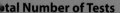

- A 50-game suspension for a positive drug test costs the average baseball player approximately $700,000 in lost salary.

Annual Prevalence of Steroid Use Among 8th, 10th, and 12th Graders

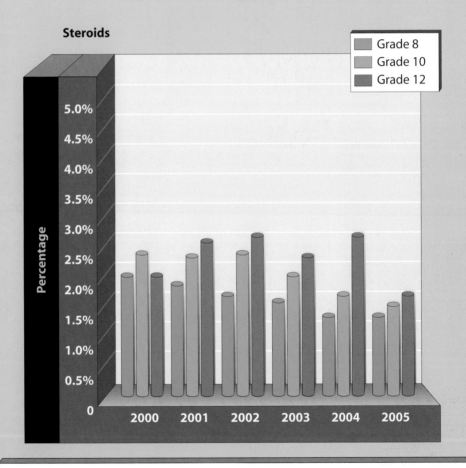

Steroid use by 8th and 10th graders has declined since 2000; however, use of steroids by 12th graders increased significantly from 2000 to 2004 but declined 40 percent in 2005.

Source: National Institute on Drug Abuse, Research Report, August 2006.

9th Grade Girls' Steroid Use Above Boys'

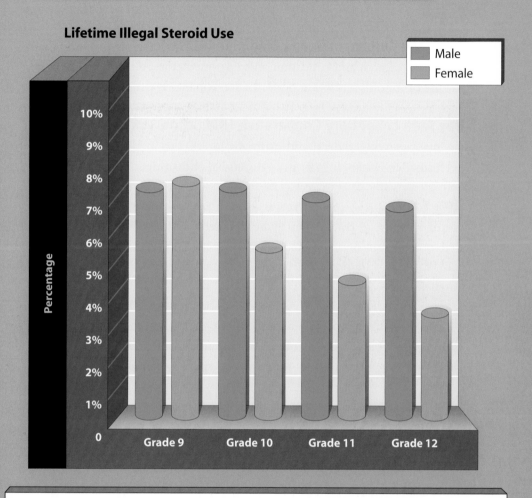

Lifetime Illegal Steroid Use

According to this survey from 2003, a higher percentage of 9th-grade girls admitted to using steroids than did boys; however, 12th-grade boys were more than twice as likely to be using steroids.

Source: Centers for Disease Control and Prevention. www.cdc.gov.

- Anabolic steroid abuse can be treated with therapy and anti-depressants.

Key People and Advocacy Groups

American College of Sports Medicine (ACSM): An organization that promotes research and education on sports medicine, ACSM seeks to stop the use of steroids and other performance-enhancing drugs in sports.

Bay Area Laboratory Cooperative (BALCO): A sports nutrition center investigated by federal authorities from 2002 to 2004 for distributing performance-enhancing drugs to dozens of elite athletes.

Jose Canseco: A former major league baseball player who wrote the autobiography *Juiced*, in which he detailed his steroid use and alleged that other prominent baseball players, including Mark McGwire, also took steroids. His book led to congressional hearings on steroid use in baseball.

Victor Conte: The founder and president of BALCO. Conte pled guilty in July 2005 to one count of conspiracy to distribute steroids and one count of money laundering, for which he spent four months in jail.

Manfred Ewald: Former head of East Germany's sports ministry and Olympic committee who oversaw East German athletes' often unknowing use of illegal performance-enhancing drugs. Ewald was convicted in 2000 of being an accessory to the intentional bodily harm of more than 100 athletes.

International Association of Athletics Federations (IAAF): The international body that governs track and field competition and oversees the drug testing of track and field athletes. Its penalties for athletes who test positive for performance-enhancing drugs are among the toughest; an athlete who tests positive twice for steroids is banned for life.

Richard Pound: Former vice president of the International Olympic Committee, currently head of the World Anti-Doping Agency and a staunch critic of the drug testing policies instituted by the four major professional sports leagues.

Robert Voy: Former chief medical officer for the United States Olympic Committee and an outspoken critic of current drug enforcement policy.

Charles Yesalis: A doctor who has extensively researched performance-enhancing drugs, including topics such as psychological dependence and the connection between steroid use and violent behavior. He has written or edited several books on the subject.

John Ziegler: The physician who created the steroid methandrostenolone, better known as Dianobol, in 1956. More powerful than testosterone, Dianobol was widely used by weightlifters and bodybuilders.

Chronology

8th Century BC
Ancient Greek athletes eat sheep testicles to improve their athletic performance.

1896
Morphine reportedly causes the death of cyclist Arthur Lindon.

1930s:
Testosterone is isolated and produced synthetically.

1960
At the Olympic Games in Rome, cyclist Knut Jensen collapses during a race and dies of a fractured skull. An autopsy reveals that he had taken stimulants.

1967
British cyclist Tommy Simpson dies during the Tour de France. Testing reveals amphetamines in his system. The IOC adds steroids to its list of banned substances.

A.D.

700 B.C.   1850   1900   1930   1940   1950   1960

1855
Cocaine is extracted from coca leaves.

1904
U.S. Olympian Tom Hicks collapses and nearly dies after winning the marathon. During the race, his trainers had given him a mixture of brandy, cocaine, and strychnine, a deadly poison.

1962
The International Olympic Committee initiates the first ban on performance-enhancing drugs.

1957
The American Medical Association issues warning to athletes about amphetamine abuse.

1874
Heroin is created. During the 19th century runners and cyclists combine cocaine and heroin to improve their endurance.

1966
The International Amateur Athletic Federation (IAAF) announces random drug testing for track and field competitions during Olympic games and European Championships.

1972
At the Olympic Games in Munich, U.S. swimmer Rick DeMont tests positive for ephedrine due to taking a prescription asthma medication. He becomes the first athlete to lose a medal because of a positive drug test.

2003
A new steroid, THG, is identified when a coach anonymously sends a syringe containing the substance to the U.S. Anti-Doping Agency; authorities raid the Bay Area Laboratory Cooperative (BALCO).

Several players from MLB and the NFL testify before Congress as part of hearings on steroids.

1999
The World Conference on Doping creates the World Anti-Doping Agency.

1987
The National Football League begins testing its athletes for steroids.

1989
The NFL begins suspending athletes who fail drug tests.

| 1975 | 1980 | 1985 | 1990 | 1995 | 2000 | 2005 |

1983
The NBA starts testing players for drug use.

2002
Major League Baseball agrees to test for steroids in the 2003 season.

2004
MLB starts suspending and fining players who test positive for steroids and bans androstenedione.

1988
Canadian sprinter Ben Johnson tests positive for steroids after winning the men's 100-meter race at the Olympics in Seoul.

2006
Fifty-six riders are removed from the Tour de France before the race begins due to evidence of doping; tour winner Floyd Landis tests positive for testosterone.

Olympic gold medal winner and world record holder of the 100-meter dash Justin Gatlin tests positive for testosterone and other steroids.

1998
The Festina cycling team is disqualified from the Tour de France when EPO is found in a team car.

Related Organizations

Athletes Training & Learning to Avoid Steroids (ATLAS)

Oregon Health & Science University

3181 SW Sam Jackson Park Rd., CR110

Portland, OR 97239-3098

phone: (503) 494-8051

fax: (503) 494-1310

e-mail: hpsm@ohsu.edu

Web site: www.atlasprogram.com

Athletes Training & Learning to Avoid Steroids targets male adolescent athletes' use of anabolic steroids and sport supplements, while also seeking to encourage healthy nutrition and exercise practices. The ATLAS program is administered by coaches and peer instructors.

Canadian Centre for Ethics in Sport (CCES)

2197 Riverside Dr., Suite 202

Ottawa, ON K1H 7X3, Canada

phone: (613) 521-3340 or (800) 672-7775

fax: (613) 521-3134

e-mail: info@cces.ca

Web site: www.cces.ca

CCES is an organization that administers drug tests in Canadian athletic programs. Educational materials and annual reports are available on its Web site. The center also publishes research papers such as "Ethical Challenges and Responsibilities Regarding Supplements."

International Association of Athletics Federations (IAAF)

17 rue Princesse Florestine, BP 359

MC98007, Monaco

phone: 011-377-93 10 8888

fax: 011-377-93 15 9515

e-mail: info@iaaf.org

Web site: www.iaaf.org

Founded in 1912, the IAAF is the governing body for track and field. It oversees an extensive drug-testing program that tests athletes both in and out of competition. The Web site features a section on drugs in sports. IAAF also publishes *IAAF Magazine.*

International Olympic Committee (IOC)

Château de Vidy, 1007

Lausanne, Switzerland

phone: 011-41-21-621-6111

fax: 011-41-21-621-6216

Web site: www.olympic.org

The IOC oversees the Olympic Games. Its antidoping code prohibits athletes from using performance-enhancing drugs.

National Center for Drug Free Sport

810 Baltimore Ave.

Kansas City, MO 64105

phone: (816) 474-8655

e-mail: info@drugfreesport.com

Web site: www.drugfreesport.com

The National Center for Drug Free Sport was founded in 1999 as a national resource for athletic organizations. It manages most aspects of the National Collegiate Athletic Association's (NCAA) drug-testing program. The center also publishes the quarterly magazine *Insight.*

National Collegiate Athletic Association (NCAA)

700 W. Washington St.,

Indianapolis, IN 46206-6222

phone: (317) 917-6222

fax: (317) 917-6888

Web site: www.ncaa.org

The NCAA oversees intercollegiate athletic programs. With the partnership of the National Center for Drug Free Sport, it also provides drug-testing and drug education programs.

National Strength and Conditioning Association

1885 Bob Johnson Dr.

Colorado Springs, CO 80906

phone: (719) 632-6722

fax: (719) 632-6367

e-mail: nsca@nsca-lift.org

Web site: www.nsca-lift.org

The purpose of the association, which consists of professionals from the health, fitness, athletic, and sports science industries, is to facilitate an exchange of ideas related to strength training and conditioning practices. It offers career certifications, educational texts and videos, and several publications, including the bimonthly journal *Strength and Conditioning*, the quarterly *Journal of Strength and Conditioning Research*, the monthly web-based publication *NSCA Performance Training Journal*, and the bimonthly newsletter *NSCA Bulletin*. Papers and position statements are available on its Web site.

United States Anti-Doping Agency (USADA)

1330 Quail Lake Loop, Suite 260

Colorado Springs, CO 80906-4651

phone: (866) 601-2632

Web site: www.usantidoping.org

The U.S. Anti-Doping Agency is dedicated to preserving the well-being of Olympic sport and the integrity of competition, and ensuring the health of athletes. The USADA focuses on four primary areas: research, education, testing, and results management.

United States Olympic Committee (USOC)

1 Olympic Plaza

Colorado Springs, CO 80909

phone: (719) 632-5551

e-mail: media@usoc.org

Web site: www.usoc.org

The U.S. Olympic Committee is a federally chartered nonprofit corporation that oversees U.S. Olympic teams and works to discourage the use of drugs in sports.

World Anti-Doping Agency (WADA)

Stock Exchange Tower

800 Place Victoria, Suite 1700

Montreal, QC H4Z 1B7, Canada

phone: (514) 904-9232

e-mail: info@wada-ama.org

Web site: www.wada-ama.org

The World Anti-Doping Agency was established by the International Olympic Committee to promote, coordinate, and monitor the fight against doping in sport in all its forms. WADA coordinated the development and implementation of the World Anti-Doping Code. Information on banned substances and drug-testing laboratories is available on its Web site. WADA publishes annual reports, the magazine *Play True*, and the newsletter *Athlete Passport*.

Web Sites

International Federation of Sports Medicine (FIMS) (www.fims. org). The International Federation of Sports Medicine is an international organization composed of national sports medicine associations that span all five continents. The aim of FIMS is to assist athletes in achieving optimal performance by maximizing their genetic potential, health, nutrition, and high-quality medical care and training.

MedLine Plus: Anabolic Steroids (www.nlm.nih.gov). Produced by the National Library of Medicine, this Web site provides information on the health risks of steroids and the use of steroids by teenagers and offers links to drug enforcement and anti–drug abuse organizations.

National Institute on Drug Abuse: Steroid Abuse Web Site (www.steroidabuse.org). This Web site, which is a public education initiative of the National Institute on Drug Abuse and several partners, including the National Collegiate Athletic Association, provides information on the dangers of anabolic steroids.

Steroid Law (www.steroidlaw.com). This Web site is run by Rick Collins, a criminal defense attorney and former bodybuilder who believes that the health risks of steroids have been exaggerated. The site supports the reform of steroid laws and provides health and legal information about steroids.

For Further Research

Books

David Aretha, *Steroids and Other Performance-Enhancing Drugs.* Berkeley Heights, NJ: MyReportLinks.com, 2005.

Michael S. Bahrke and Charles E. Yesalis, eds., *Performance-Enhancing Substances in Sport and Exercise.* Champaign, IL: Human Kinetics, 2002.

Howard Bryant, *Juicing the Game: Drugs, Power, and the Fight for the Soul of Major League Baseball.* New York: Viking, 2005.

Jose Canseco, *Juiced: Wild Times, Rampant 'Roids, Smash Hits, and How Baseball Got Big.* New York: Regan Books, 2005.

Will Carroll, *The Juice: The Real Story of Baseball's Drug Problems.* Chicago: Ivan R. Dee, 2005.

Rick Collins, *Legal Muscle: Anabolics in America.* East Meadow, NY: Legal Muscle, 2002.

Mark Fainaru-Wada and Lance Williams, *Game of Shadows: Barry Bonds, BALCO, and the Steroids Scandal That Rocked Professional Sports.* New York: Gotham, 2006.

Karla Fitzhugh, *Steroids.* Chicago: Heinemann Library, 2005.

John Hoberman, *Testosterone Dreams: Rejuvenation, Aphrodisia, and Doping.* Berkeley and Los Angeles: University of California Press, 2005.

Cynthia Kuhn, Scott Swartzwelder, and Wilkie Wilson, *Pumped: Straight Facts for Athletes About Drugs, Supplements and Training.* New York: Norton, 2000.

Pat Lenehan, *Anabolic Steroids: And Other Performance-Enhancing Drugs.* New York: Taylor and Francis, 2003.

Suzanne Levert, *The Facts About Steroids.* Tarrytown, NY: Benchmark, 2005.

John McCloskey and Julian Bailes, *When Winning Costs Too Much: Steroids, Supplements, and Scandal in Today's Sports World.* Lanham, MD: Taylor Trade, 2005.

Judy Monroe, *Steroids, Sports, and Body Image: The Risks of Performance-Enhancing Drugs*. Berkeley Heights, NJ: Enslow, 2004.

David R. Mottram, *Drugs in Sport*. London: Routledge, 2005.

Greg Shepard, *Bigger, Faster, Stronger*. Champaign, IL: Human Kinetics, 2004.

Albert Spring, *Steroids and Your Muscles: The Incredible Disgusting Story*. New York: Rosen Central, 2001.

William N. Taylor, *Anabolic Steroids and the Athlete*. Jefferson, NC: McFarland, 2002.

———, *Anabolic Therapy in Modern Medicine*. Jefferson, NC: McFarland, 2002.

Steven Ungerleider, *Faust's Gold: Inside the East German Doping Machine*. New York: St. Martin's, 2001.

Ivan Waddington, *Sport, Health, and Drugs*. New York: Routledge, 2000.

Wayne Wilson and Edward Derse, eds., *Doping in Elite Sport: The Politics of Drugs in the Olympic Movement*. Champaign, IL: Human Kinetics, 2001.

Charles E. Yesalis, *Performance-Enhancing Substances in Sport and Exercise*. Champaign, IL: Human Kinetics, 2002.

Periodicals

Jacqueline Adams, "The Incredible Bulk," *Science World*, March 28, 2005.

Jerry Adler, "Toxic Strength," *Newsweek*, December 20, 2004.

Wayne M. Barrett, "Why the Incredible Hulk Is Batting Cleanup," *USA Today* magazine, May 2004.

Kim Clark and Robert Milliken, "Positive on Testing," *U.S. News & World Report*, August 14, 2000.

Glenn Cook, "Shortcut to Tragedy," *American School Board Journal*, August 2004.

Brian Duffy, "Why Cutting Corners Comes as No Surprise," *U.S. News & World Report*, August 7, 2006.

Economist, "Drugs and the Olympics," August 7, 2004.

———, "Ever Farther, Ever Faster, Ever Higher?" August 7, 2004.

Malcolm Gladwell, "Drugstore Athlete," *New Yorker*, September 10, 2001.

Bengt Kayser, Alexandre Mauron, and Andy Miah, "Viewpoint: Legalisation of Performance-Enhancing Drugs," *Lancet*, December 17, 2005.

Jeffrey Kluger, "The Steroid Detective," *Time*, March 1, 2004.

Kathiann M. Kowalski, "Performance-Enhancing Drugs: The Truth Behind the Hype," *Current Health 2*, February 2003.

Michael Le Page, "Only Drugs Can Stop the Sports Cheats," *New Scientist*, August 19, 2006.

Frank Litsky, "Criticism Is Leveled at U.S. Drug Testing," *New York Times*, February 5, 2002.

Stephen Pincock, "Feature: Gene Doping," *Lancet*, December 17, 2005.

James Poniewozik, "This Is Your Nation on Steroids," *Time*, December 20, 2004.

Rick Reilly, "The 'Roid to Ruin," *Sports Illustrated*, August 21, 2000.

Steven Shapin, "Cleanup Hitters," *New Yorker*, April 18, 2005.

Mark Starr, "Blowing the Whistle on Drugs," *Newsweek*, November 3, 2003.

———, "Tackling the Pros," *Newsweek*, December 20, 2004.

Steven Ungerleider, "Steroids: Youth at Risk," *Harvard Mental Health Letter*, May 2001.

Tom Verducci, "Is This the Asterisk Era?" *Sports Illustrated*, March 15, 2004.

Weekly Reader, "Steroids Are the Rage," January 16, 2004.

David Wharton, "Voice of Dissent in Drug Wars," *Los Angeles Times*, May 9, 2004.

Randall R. Wroble, Michael Gray, and Joseph A. Rodrigo, "Anabolic Steroids and Pre-Adolescent Athletes," *Sport Journal*, Fall 2002.

Internet Sources

John Doe (hidden witness), "The Abuse of Anabolic Steroids and Their Precursors by Adolescent and Amateur Athletes," Senate Caucus on International Narcotics Control, July 13, 2004. http://drugcaucus. senate.gov/steroids04doe.html.

Healthy Competition, "The Blue Cross and Blue Shield Association's Healthy Competition Foundation Position on Creatine Supplementation." www.healthycompetition.org.

National Institute on Drug Abuse, "NIDA InfoFacts: Steroids (Anabolic-Androgenic)." www.drugabuse.gov/infofacts/steroids.html.

Julian Savulescu, Bennett Foddy, and Megan Clayton, "Why We Should Allow Performance Enhancing Drugs in Sport," *British Journal of Sports Medicine Online*, 2004. http://bjsm.bmjjournals.com/cgi/content/full/38/6/666.

World Anti-Doping Agency, "World Anti-Doping Code." www.wada-ama.org/en/dynamic.ch2?pageCategory.id=250.

Source Notes

Overview: Performance-Enhancing Drugs in Modern Athletics

1. Malcolm Gladwell, "Drugstore Athlete," *New Yorker*, September 10, 2001, p. 54.
2. Greg Schwab, testimony before the U.S. Senate Subcommittee on Consumer Affairs, Foreign Commerce, and Tourism, June 18, 2002, p. 30.
3. Jon Saraceno, "Jones Has Run Out of Excuses," *USA Today*, August 23, 2006.
4. John Hoberman, "The Testers Can't Win," *Guardian* (Manchester), August 1, 2006. www.guardian.co.uk.

Is the Use of Performance-Enhancing Drugs Cheating?

5. John Hoberman, "The Testers Can't Win," *Guardian* (Manchester), August 1, 2006.
6. Howard Bryant, *Juicing the Game: Drugs, Power, and the Fight for the Soul of Major League Baseball.* New York: Viking, 2005, p. 103.
7. Bryant, *Juicing the Game*, p. 140.
8. George W. Bush, State of the Union address, January 20, 2004.
9. Steve Yuhas, "Steroid Scandal Overblown and Hypocritical—Congress and Teams Ought Not Be So Self-Righteous," December 14, 2004. www.politics.com.
10. Julian Savulescu, Bennett Foddy, and Megan Clayton, "Why We Should Allow Performance Enhancing Drugs in Sport," *British Journal of Sports Medicine*, 2004, p. 667.
11. Sidney Gendin, "Let's Ban Those Who Don't Use Drugs," Fall 2000. http://meso-rx.com.

12. Charles E. Yesalis and Virginia S. Cowart, *The Steroids Game.* Champaign, IL:Human Kinetics, 1998, p. 110.

How Dangerous Are Performance-Enhancing Drugs?

13. Bryant, *Juicing the Game*, p. 177.
14. Bryant, *Juicing the Game*, p. 146.
15. Drug Enforcement Administration, *Steroid Abuse in Today's Society,* March 2004, p. 8.
16. Rick Collins, "Health Risks of Anabolic Steroids," 1999. www.steroidlaw.com.
17. Michael Le Page, "Only Drugs Can Stop the Sports Cheats," *New Scientist*, August 19, 2006, pp. 18–19.
18. Bengt Kayser, Alexandre Mauron, and Andy Miah, "Viewpoint: Legalisation of Performance-Enhancing Drugs," *Lancet*, December 17, 2005, p. S21.
19. Philippe Liotard, "Sport Medicine: To Heal or to Win?" *UNESCO Courier*, September 2000, p. 39.
20. Maxwell J. Mehlman, "Performance Enhancing Drugs in Sports," The Doctor Will See You Now. www.thedoctorwillseeyounow.com.

How Effective Is Testing for Performance-Enhancing Drugs?

21. Jack L. Copeland, "Drug Testing Program Withstanding the Test of Time," *NCAA News*, September 30, 2002. www.ncaa.org.
22. Bud Selig, statement before the U.S. House Committee on Government Reform, March 17, 2005.
23. Malcolm Gladwell, "Drugstore Athlete," *New Yorker*, September 10, 2001.

How Can the Use of Performance-Enhancing Drugs Be Prevented?

24. Bob Goldman and Ronald Klatz, *Death in the Locker Room II: Drugs and Sports*. Chicago: Elite Sports Publications, 1992, p. 24.
25. Paul Tagliabue, testimony before the U.S. House Subcommittee on Commerce, Trade, and Consumer Protection, March 18–19, 2005, p. 100.
26. Merrell Noden, "A Great Ugly Cloud," *Sports Illustrated*, September 7, 1998, p. 29.
27. Antonio Davis, testimony before the U.S. Senate Committee on Commerce, Science, and Transportation, September 28, 2005, p. 3.
28. Doug Bandow, "Busybodies on Steroids," *American Spectator*, December 10, 2004. www.spectator.org.

List of Illustrations

Index

About the Author

San Diego resident Laura K. Egendorf received her BA in English from Wesleyan University. A book editor for the past nine years, she is especially interested in books that explore free speech or popular culture. When she is not working, Laura's interests include food, sports, music, and trivia.